ANOTHER ENGLISH

POETRY

FOUNDATION

Another English: Anglophone Poems from Around the World is part of a collaboration with the *Poets in the World* series created by the Poetry Foundation's Harriet Monroe Poetry Institute. The *Poets in the World* series supports research and publication of poetry and poetics from around the world and highlights the importance of creating space for poetry in local communities.

THE HARRIET MONROE POETRY INSTITUTE

is an independent forum created by the Poetry Foundation to provide a space in which fresh thinking about poetry, in both its intellectual and practical needs, can flourish free of allegiances other than to the best ideas. The Institute convenes leading poets, scholars, publishers, educators, and other thinkers from inside and outside the poetry world to address issues of importance to the art form of poetry and to identify and champion solutions for the benefit of the art.

Visit www.poetryfoundation.org/institute

THE POETRY FOUNDATION,

publisher of *Poetry* magazine, is an independent literary organization committed to a vigorous presence for poetry in our culture. It exists to discover and celebrate the best poetry and to place it before the largest possible audience. The Poetry Foundation seeks to be a leader in shaping a receptive climate for poetry by developing new audiences, creating new avenues for delivery, and encouraging new kinds of poetry through innovative partnerships, prizes, and programs.

Visit www.poetryfoundation.org

Another English

ANGLOPHONE POEMS
FROM AROUND
THE WORLD

EDITED BY
CATHERINE BARNETT AND
TIPHANIE YANIQUE

WITH REGIONAL CURATORS
HINEMOANA BAKER, KWAME DAWES,
ISHION HUTCHINSON, RUSTUM KOZAIN,
LES MURRAY, SUDEEP SEN,
AND TODD SWIFT

POETRY
FOUNDATION

POETRY FOUNDATION'S
HARRIET MONROE POETRY INSTITUTE
ILYA KAMINSKY, POETS IN THE WORLD SERIES EDITOR

T|P TUPELO PRESS

This book is a co-publication of Tupelo Press and The Poetry Foundation,
produced as part of the *Poets in the World* series
created by The Poetry Foundation's Harriet Monroe Poetry Institute.
Cover and text design by Josef Beery.
Butterfly images from period natural history publications.
First edition, April 2014.

Another English : Anglophone Poems from Around the World / edited by Catherine Barnett
and Tiphanie Yanique ; with regional curators Hinemoana Baker, Kwame Dawes, Ishion
Hutchinson, Rustum Kozain, Les Murray, Sudeep Sen, and Todd Swift. -- First edition.
    pages cm. -- (Poets in the World Series)
        ISBN 978-1-936797-40-0 (pbk. original : alk. paper)
    1. Commonwealth poetry (English) 2. English poetry--English-speaking countries.
        I. Barnett, Catherine, editor of compilation.
        II. Yanique, Tiphanie, editor of compilation.
                PR9086.A55 2014
                821--dc23
                                        2013046099

Tupelo Press is an award-winning independent literary press that publishes fine fiction,
nonfiction, and poetry in books that are a joy to hold as well as read. Tupelo Press is a
registered 501(c)(3) nonprofit organization, and we rely on public support to carry out
our mission of publishing extraordinary work that may be outside the realm of large
commercial publishers. Financial donations are welcome and are tax deductible.

*Published with support of The Poetry Foundation and
the National Endowment for the Arts.*

English
Is my mother tongue.

A mother tongue is not
not a foreign lan lan lang
language
l/anguish
anguish
— a foreign anguish.

   —M. NourbeSe Philip

As humanity is one under its amazing diversities,
language is one under its.

   —Walt Whitman

Contents

Editors' Introduction

What excited us most was the clamor this book might become: how it might, though called an "anthology," resist conventionality and respectability and be experienced instead as "You need to know about this—and this, and this too," unfolding like a series of greetings.

The basic idea was that international poets would choose, from their countries of origin, a small but mighty collection of the English-language poems they consider essential reading. This was to be an artist's approach, and to that end we enlisted the insights of seven bright sparks, each an award-winning poet in his or her own right: Kwame Dawes (Ghana), Ishion Hutchinson (the Caribbean), Rustum Kozain (South Africa), Les Murray (Australia), Hinemoana Baker (New Zealand), Sudeep Sen (India), and Todd Swift (Canada).

We wanted to know what our regional curators' poetic welcomings would do to our sense of the English language and how they might enlarge our appreciation for world poetry, rendering us less myopic, provincial, and chauvinistic.

This project is one of the many set in motion by the poet and translator Ilya Kaminsky during his time as director of the Poetry Foundation's Harriet Monroe Poetry Institute. When Ilya asked us to serve as editors, he referred to this simply as an anthology of "Anglophone" poetry, and we agreed without quite understanding just how complicated, vexed, and useful, yet at the same time almost useless, the word "Anglophone" can be. Suffice it to say that the longer we work on this book, the vexier this term has come to be.

For example, we quickly realized that the seven commissioned regional anthologies, as diverse and provocative as they were, were woefully inadequate as a representation of contemporary Anglophone poetry. But to have been comprehensive, the book would have billowed to unwieldy proportions. Consider that there are eighty-plus sovereign states and territories where English is an official or predominant language; in this book we have included poems from a small fraction of that number and still weigh in at many pages. And needless to say, the task of choosing just a sampling of poems out of the thousands of terrific poems from any one region demands repeated and necessary apologies. Each poet-curator lamented the built-in constraints of the assignment; none claims that his or her selections are the "best" but only that these are poems that are far too often unknown to American readers.

As editors, we've fortified ourselves, and we hope you will, too, in contending with this assembly of praise, diversity, and wild idiosyncrasy, by remembering what Einstein said about limitations: "Once we accept our limits we go beyond them."

The very concept of a global Anglophone poetics is problematic and politicized. In every case, the countries presented here use English because the British have colonized them. In some cases English was historically considered an oppressor language; in some cases English is not the only national or even the most vital language. In the Canadian selections, for example, we've had to exclude the Francophone poets. In the Caribbean, we've omitted French-, Spanish-, and Dutch-language poets. In South Africa, where English is lingua franca, there are situations where English-speaking poets have chosen to write in Afrikaans or Xhosa as a form of ethno-political identification and action. And India has a long literary history—poets were publishing in Urdu and Hindi well before the British arrived—yet we could not include Urdu and Hindi in an English-language anthology. These concessions to our "Anglophone" premise, and dozens of others, pain us.

But each time we looked back at the proposed poems, and as we considered the passion and eloquence of the curator-poets who selected poems to represent their regions, we felt rejuvenated and determined to find a way to make this anthology work, remembering its simple mandate: to bring together into one book of poems a collection of varied expressions of English. Of Englishes born and thriving in disparate places. Of Englishes inflected and charged by various cultures, languages, politics, and histories. We think you'll hear tremendous variety in these selections—in the way the poems slip at times between standard and colloquial, between uttered and professed, between sung and stated, between praise and lament.

There are so many poets Calibaning these Englishes, thereby making the language(s) bounce and burst, poets not only from England and the United States—the perceived homes of English—but from far away and nearby, from beautiful geographies of land, mind, and voice that are at once fiercely independent and, through the medium of poetry, intimately interwoven.

To illuminate what are wonderfully complex and rich aspects of the English language—its manifold expressions, its malleability and resilience and subterfuges and fragility, and, as with all languages, its failures—we've structured the anthology to accommodate the kinds of partnerings and independences that national and regional boundaries create. Our regions are sometimes nations in and of themselves, separated by vast geographical distances—India, Canada, South Africa, and Ghana, for example. In "The Antipodes," we present Australia and New Zealand both as individual countries and as an inter-related region that shares a geographical domain and also sometimes shares poets; for instance, Jennifer Compton, born in New Zealand but represented here under Australia, where she has lived most of her life. Similarly, we present a diverse representation of the countries and territories of the Caribbean—The Bahamas, Barbados, Guyana, Jamaica, Montserratt, Trinidad and Tobago, Saint Lucia, Saint Vincent and the Grenadines, and the Virgin Islands—places held together by the sometimes-boundary/sometimes-bridge that is the Caribbean archipelago.

Our hope and belief is that this organization will allow the varieties of English to face and complement and challenge each other within close geographical proximity and across much greater distances of every kind.

We anticipate that there will be sequels to this anthology, volumes that can include Nigeria, Kenya, Bangladesh, Pakistan, Papua New Guinea, the Pacific Islands and the islands in the Indian Ocean, more of the Caribbean; perhaps a future anthology might include Grenada, the British Virgin Islands, Saint Kitts and Nevis, Antigua, Dominica, and Puerto Rico. Comparable rectifications await in every part of the Anglophone world.

Yet let's not look at all that isn't here, but relish all that is: these poems come to us by grace of the eyes and ears of our discerning artist-curators, who are each actively making their own poems along with teaching and compiling other anthologies, while generously taking the time to share their enthusiasms here and in the process enlarging a landscape and language-scape that poetry readers in the United States often overlook or fail to comprehend.

We like to think of this book as an "anthology of anthologies," and with that in mind, we'll introduce the regional curators to whom we are greatly indebted:

Kwame Dawes, who curates the poems from Ghana, where he was born (although a poem of his own is included in the selection from the Caribbean, where he has lived), speaks of "Empathy as a function of the imagination," a notion that characterizes his choices. "I happen to think that a poem's strength must involve some kind of risk, something that makes the poem urgent. And yes, I think that the poem should reveal us in some way." The poems he has chosen beseech us to pay attention. Kofi Awoonor's "Sea Time," for instance, is a beautiful example of one of the many varieties of empathy found in Dawes's selections. Dedicated to a friend expected to die by firing squad, and written while Awoonor himself was in prison, "Sea Time" presents us with a prisoner's inventory: the smuggled egg, the memories remembered again and again. Awoonor commits this seemingly quiet poem as "a garland / for your wounded knees," a clear empathetic gesture. He knows what his friend is going through, for he is going through this himself, and Dawes, by including poems of such great immediacy, awakens us to the largest human concerns in a country's tumultuous recent history.

In the poems gathered for the Caribbean sections, words seem to rise right out of the region's earth and water, as in Shara McCallum's "What the Oracle Said" and in "XII" from Dionne Brand's sequence "Land to Light On." Both poems suggest that the loss of one's native environs parallels losing one's most intimate self. "We have a society that is inventing itself out of the fissures of things that have survived the worst of human tragedy," says section curator and poet **Ishion Hutchison**, who enlisted the help of five other poets and writers—**Andre Bagoo, Christian Campbell, Kendel Hippolyte, Nicholas Laughlin**, and this book's coeditor **Tiphanie Yanique**—to gather a double selection from the Caribbean nations. In these poems we see that the Caribbean, a region plagued by slavery, colonialism, and natural disaster, is in great creative flux, perhaps because of the diversity of voices and postures that has risen above the tragedies.

Rustum Kozain, a poet, teacher, and editor, has arranged his selection of poems from South Africa in chronological order; the poems date from 1970 to 1998 and create a map of South African poetry responding aggressively to apartheid during those years. His selections can be read as a conversation among poets publishing at that time, a conversation about revolt and revolution reflecting both the personal aspects, as seen especially in Ingrid de Kok's poems, and the protest aspects, as seen in Chris van Wyk's "In Detention" and other poems. In a public letter Kozain wrote to Nelson Mandela to celebrate Mandela's ninetieth birthday, Kozain asserts, "It is no surprise that, in a country where the (black/white) body was the main principle of political organisation, one can feel politics right down into the blood and bone. One can experience politics with all the tragic depression of heart-break." The poems Kozain has chosen inhabit and speak from blood and bone.

In his essay "In Defense of Poetry," **Les Murray**, who selected our Australian poems, makes a case for poetry as a fundamental part of the human experience, "the standard equipment of the human soul." As a poet and as an editor, Murray is interested in questions: "What does some phenomenon in the world mean? What does it lead to, what does it point to, what deeper dimension can you find in it?" He asks himself and his readers: "What is the poem of your life?" In his section of Australian poetry, the poems—"fitted for the spirit's explorations"—record the intimate and necessary stories we humans tell ourselves. Murray says he himself tries to be a "disobedient poet," and we feel some of that respect for disobedience in his choices and also in his brief introduction, in which he argues against category, definition, or commentary, preferring to let the poems speak for themselves.

"It would be safe to say that we haven't been a country that really embraces and celebrates our artists as much as we celebrate and embrace our rugby players," says **Hinemoana Baker**, who selected our fifteen New Zealand poems. "I think that's slowly changing." A singer as well as a poet, Baker chose poems that are meant to be heard and not just read; their insistence originates in their music, their humor, and their "issues of justice, right and wrong," which Baker privileges as she highlights poems that come "from those times when you're asking questions and not knowing all the answers."

"The architecture of a poem is very important to me," writes **Sudeep Sen**, a poet and anthologist whose selections in English by Indians draw from contemporary poets who are inventing new forms and playing with and against tradition. Like others of our regional curators, Sen is aware that "In the postcolonial literary scene, poets and novelists writing in English from the non-English-speaking world do suffer, in most cases, from a sense of displacement." He notes the power of this phenomenon in the writings from the South Asian diaspora. Sen's selections underscore his claim that "there's a confidence in the language, an unabashedness. One or two generations ago English was a postcolonial language. It's no longer the case. For me, English is an Indian language. It is one of our twenty-six official languages." He leans toward what he calls "the power in understated writing," pushing against the superficial and against poems "that sound like statements, as if the only aim of poetry is to give expression to a set of ideas or agendas."

Todd Swift, the curator of our Canada selections, urges "compassion, eclectic reading habits, and a willingness to appreciate the polar opposite." You'll find among his poems a tension—"between excess and austerity . . . where poems occur." Swift is also a screenwriter, and we see that he relied on his cinematic eye to choose poems that "warn, worry, but ultimately heal." Resonating with other work gathered here, these fifteen Canadian poems should not (as Swift says of all good poetry) "be marketed only as entertainment, but as something ubiquitous and necessary, like water."

So it turns out that yes, this is a "You need to know this and this" kind of book, and yes it's a series of greetings—the kind of greeting you experience when you walk into someone's living room or study and get a feel for his or her tastes, experiences, particular passions. We've come to see each regional gathering here as a room for you to walk through, where the poems are like paintings and wall hangings and artifacts awaiting your encounter.

We've attempted to leave the initial encounter as untrammeled by explication as possible, so you'll find the collections of poems on their own in the first half of the book, followed by a "Curators' Forum: Notes and Commentary on the Selections," in which each regional curator provides some contextual information about the

writers and their countries to accompany the poems. We hope read-
ers will travel out of the rooms that are most familiar to them and
into rooms where they'll hear exciting, unforeseen forms of English.

We are grateful to Ilya Kaminsky for dreaming up and then
remaining steadfastly supportive of this project, and we thank our
brilliant curators for their hard work, intelligence, grace, generosity
of spirit, and breadth of knowledge. May their selections serve as
both windows and mirrors.

—*Catherine Barnett and Tiphanie Yanique*

Editors' Acknowledgments

*We'd like especially to thank—in every language and in every variety of
English—Ilya Kaminsky, Beth Allen, and Tupelo managing editor Jim
Schley for bringing this unruly anthology not only into existence but into
shape. Their vision, patience, and good humor are models for us all, and
they accompanied us across the oceans and continents. We would like
to take one last moment to say another world-resounding thank you to
the regional curators for your shepherding and your thoughtful, brilliant
responses to our admittedly difficult mission. Which brings us to the
poets themselves, in whose company we have been delighted and moved
to find ourselves over these years. Thank you to the New School for bring-
ing us together as colleagues, and thank you to the Poetry Foundation
for entrusting us with this project. Behind the scenes, Laura Jo Hess,
Phillippa Yaa de Villiers, Jessica Kovler, and Lucy Gardner Carson pro-
vided essential research and review, and we are indebted to them for their
gracious intelligence. Finally, thank you to our families who were patient
as we struggled and strove to bring this anthology to fruition.*

ONE

AN ANTHOLOGY OF ANTHOLOGIES
THE POEMS

GHANA

CURATED BY KWAME DAWES

WIDESPREAD FORESTER
EUPHAEDRA MEDON

KWADWO OPOKU-AGYEMANG

In the Dungeon

You guessed it
A castle is a dream
Without windows

There are dogs, wet-eyed
Without owners

A slave is as naked
As a peeled vein
In a dream

The dust dies on the turrets
From thirst and tiredness

We buried dust inland
With anger and a voice
And a dozen brave words

Full of sugary sap
And a national anthem
The young voices
Salute their future with
"I am not worthy, Holy Lord"

There is a chill
And it is not over yet

KWADWO OPOKU-AGYEMANG
Cape Coast Town

You can tell
By the way it leans
Exhausted
The erect ambitions
It has weathered

My life flows seaward
A slow day-dream dissolving
With the irrational streets
The back-handed charm
The night-mud houses
Their eyes half-shut

An aged town
It stands on the one good foot
Shaking and forgetful

What matters
Is not just the ruins
Or the years devouring one another
But the veins
That still escape with the blood

KWESI BREW

Adam and Eve and the New Paradise

His bed was softened with petals of lilies
Plucked from the fields of Elysium
Where he was wont to take his evening walk
And shout for Adam and enquire of Eve.
But all that was before the Revolution
Now he sleeps on a bed of nails;
The garden has run to weed
And there is no Adam to hail, nor Eve to enquire of.

Having grabbed a sizable portion of the national cake,
Thoroughly scrubbed the blood clean from his hands
Adam had gone north to protect his gains,
Leaving Eve, Abel, and Cain to fend for themselves
With what portions they could get in the scramble.
That was when Adam thought God had died
Because he never called there
Where Adam was to enquire of him.

Eve of Eves whom corruption does not corrupt
Nor extravagance taint,
Had built for herself a new heaven on a new earth.
She had moved south to the great Market
To sell seersucker and Dutch wax prints and organza and damask
And necklaces and earrings that looked very much like gold.
The garden homestead, now deserted, is used for synods and conventions.
By a communion of crows.

KOFI AWOONOR
My God of Songs Was Ill

Go and tell them that I crossed the river
While the canoes were still empty
And the boatman had gone away.
My god of songs was ill
And I was taking him to be cured.
When I went the fetish priest was away
So I waited outside the hut
My god of songs was groaning
Crying.
I gathered courage
I knocked on the fetish hut
And the cure god said in my tongue
"Come in with your backside"
So I walked in with my backside
With my god of songs crying on my head
I placed him on the stool.
Then the bells rang and my name was called thrice
My god groaned amidst the many voices
The cure god said I had violated my god
"Take him to your father's gods"
But before they opened the hut
My god burst into songs, new strong songs
That I am still singing with him.

KOFI AWOONOR

Sea Time

(for Kojo Tsikata, sentenced to death by firing squad)

I hear the thuds again.
They just brought me a smuggled egg
   I ate it and afterwards
      belched.

The sea pelts the land
with grains of fine drops
   very cold, this August
some were talking of dying
of petitions and reprieves
Ousman speaks of his horse
He's been a thief all his life.

In 48 they held a victory dance
belatedly and I
as a boy drank too much.

We come now to the house
by the sea, to the ferry port
   Companioned by gulls
and the shouts of naked boat men
   deserters and watchmen
      at many shrines.

The wisdom that my father had
is not passed. I dreamt
my grandmother mocked me
as I led a tattered procession

of women and children
    to seek a reprieve on a road.

Go and tell them
that my passion is ended
that my love I gave away
that I need no braves
on the ferry. That if need be
    I'll row it alone
    We already spoke of cannons
    and roses; of death
    and tree gardens
    of love and milk and prison
    of an egg and tiger nuts.

I come alone into the city
    all are gone to the ferry port.
Alone here I wander among ghosts
of soldiers who died in domestic wars
Alone I sing of cannons
and rain among the memory of slaves
of life and fruit trees
hunger in alleyways
and tears, abundant tears
(oh, when shall I sing of joy alone?)

But I promise a harvest
unheard of; I promise a garland
for your wounded knees
(the ones you gained when you fell
    in the communal bathhouse)

a crown of thorns is too common
who needs a crown of thorns?

They promised me they'll come into the city
with me. They swore
They'll lead me to the festival grounds
for l have a pledge to make
I'll make it
before death comes.

My smuggler is offering eggs.
l need many eggs.

    (Ussher Fort Prison)

KOFI AWOONOR

The Weaver Bird

The weaver bird built in our house
And laid its eggs on our only tree.
We did not want to send it away.
We watched the building of the nest
And supervised the egg-laying.
And the weaver returned in the guise of the owner.
Preaching salvation to us that owned the house.
They say it came from the west
Where the storms at sea had felled the gulls
And the fishers dried their nets by lantern light.
Its sermon is the divination of ourselves
And our new horizon limit at its nest.
But we cannot join the prayers and answers of the communicants.
We look for new homes every day,
For new altars we strive to re-build
The old shrines defiled by the weaver's excrement.

AMA ATA AIDOO

Totems

I
came upon an owl
at the crossroads
blinking with confusion
greater than
mine!

Bird of doom.
Bird of promise.

Fluorescent lightning on a
city corn-field,
tell the owl of
the changing times.

They-of-the-Crow
cannot
carve out
destinies through
marriage.

Whoever can?

He does
too well by her,
          and
she always
knows when
starched rags go to swaddle
another's baby.

Dodua of the light palms:
She is hanging out the
last new to dry from its
first washing.

Perch where you can, and
tell your story. They make
us believe that all roofs
cover homes from the rain.

Akua my sister,
No one chooses to stand
under a tree in a storm.

So
You
shall not be the one to remind
Me
to keen for the great ancestors and
call to mind the ruined hamlet
that was once
the Home of Kings.

Itu kwan
ma
Adze sa wo aa
na
Adze asa wo!!!

KOJO LAING
Godhorse

The horse with birds on its mane, doubt on its tail . . .
doubt about the flies being whisked north or south . . .
crawled out of the relieved horizon, in
a burst of dung part-colored with kente.
And the angle at which the horse bisected the hills,
made it easy for the old man with the square body
to jump up its decorated left flank, leaving
half his age behind as his bones came down like a pounder.
Galloping was a definition of time, more
for the man, less for the horse
whose high brown snorting would be framed
if only there were strong hands,
if only the ancestors would jump the centuries.
Now a woman raised her right breast on the right flank
of this horse of wonder, this horse
with a mane maimed by the limiting beauty of birds.
Mansa's whole body shook — O god of soft thunder! —
as the old man stretched his lust across horse flesh,
trying to speed through the geography of tails, but
suddenly meeting ghana
               half-way up the horse instead; suddenly
seeing bishops and fetish priests
so that his reverence gently covered his lust, true
the religious men wanted to bless the imprudent hooves, but
the horse threw off angels with a burst of shank, with
the old man kneeling on the saddle and begging Mansa for love,
as her breasts shook in incense.
Since the sun and the moon were
               in a simultaneous sky,

Mansa watched half a country hang on half a horse,
          watched the old man's smiles and rejected
          each one,
throwing the most outrageous one under the hardest hoof.
Pound your laughter, pound your world!
Rejection was no different, even when mixed with speed,
old man's nails were digging into horse country,
old man's knees were shaking the shanks
          of a suddenly stationary stallion:
horse hair was full of brown regret,
          was full of the morality of not galloping
when the country was sagging with the speed of time.
But let horse dung salute accra!
Let the blue moon burst over a clear gallop!
Let them rise against the unwanted pity of horse ethics!
We want the african touch, neighed the horse, for
it desperately loved Mansa's thighs pressing against it. But
old man shouted the horse on. Onnnn!
For the half of ghana that was missing
          was merely the gaps in his old teeth,
          was merely the spatial side of galloping.
On! Human flesh orbits horse flesh!
Old man falls from flank to flank,
bouncing across a withering country, shivering
under the weight of horse decrees
          that Mansa carried on behalf of the
          authorities.
On! with the most moral horse in the world, for its
thighs did not return the pressure of Mansa's thighs, for
after all the universe was a stilled gallop,
          was an old man crawling away from a
          cantering, crazy life,

was a contradictory shank shaking.
As Mansa fell off at last by the tune of a distant highlife,
the horse snorted for other women, the
    horse . . . its morality lost in its speed at last . . .
        threw off the old man.
Man, poor, old: he died with a smile before he hit the ground:
           and under him were the crushed birds, O God,
           carrying their expanding beauty still, still.

ATUKWEI OKAI
Watu Wazuri
(to B. B. Attuquayefio)

I

When all the blue is gone out
of the sky
and the remaining hue is nothing
to fly a kite by,

birdsong
is the green lawn
of spring

on which the ears laze.

Upon the nile of my soul,
the lullaby of the flutist
floats

like a kite at dawn.

Ray Charles
and
Stevie Wonder

you are acquainted with the
laughter of thunder

but not with the look and
the smile of her lightning

that will meander

like the singing leap-year spine
of the sexy celestial belly dancer.

Like a Bobodiulasso kite
commissioned by the Supreme Council

of the clouds
and the moonlight
and the ten toes and ten fingers
of the horizon of the soul,

you only wander and wonder —

you do not see
the world
you sing about

Waumdaji,
Waumdaji
Watu Wazuri —
Rhododendrons in donkeydom.

2

Beethoven
Beethoven

you don't hear the songs
you sing about the world

Waumdaji,
Waumdaji
Watu Wazuri —
Rhododendrons in donkeydom.

3

Miriam Makeba . . .
Miriam Makeba . . .

She shall not savour
the air and the soil of the land
that fuels and fires
her soul into song.

Miriam Makeba,

her spirit shall never waver.
Lonely in the cave-canyon-kraal
of labour,

stealthily sucks
of her motherland's
midnight breasts,
bursts forth into new births of song,

steeling the spirit
of her people panting and prancing

in the dormant
volcano-dungeon

of racialist dung
and human wrong.

Waumdaji,
Waumdaji
Watu Wazuri —
Rhododendrons in donkeydom.

4

Osagyefo Kwame Nkrumah,

   O spirit on an errand,
   O spirit on an errand,

no sooner had you folded your mat
and gone beyond the corn-fields

than the victoria falls
the namib desert
and the table mountain

burst out in tears
and fire,

and the towncrier and his gong
and the eagle soaring in flight
burst out into flight and into song,

   guinea bissau, angola —
   mozambique, angola —

guinea bissau, angola —
mozambique, angola —

A LUTA CONTINUA
A LUTA CONTINUA

Waumdaji,
Waumdaji
Watu Wazuri —
Rhododendrons in donkeydom.

ISHMAEL FIIFI ANNOBIL

Rwanda

Toadstools grow
In their nostrils —
Poisoned, the soldiers —

Bats,
Pressed to
The red glint of
Blades of an
Apocalypse.

The day sun
Fell into
The river — the rainbow is off colour —
The penumbra wept
Red tears

And howled.

(Grangetown, Cardiff: 20 May 1994)

ABENA BUSIA
Caliban

This tongue that I have mastered
has mastered me;

has taught me curses
in the language of the master

has taught me bondage
in the language of the master

I speak this dispossession
in the language of the master

and I am a woman ravished and naked
chanting the words of a little girl lost
treading the edge of the waves

trying to recapture . . .

the dream of a virgin robed in moonlight
reaching gestures across the waters
singing a song of home

I'm a black man's child, still
stranded on the shores of saxon seas

A. W. KAYPER-MENSAH

Dying Birth

For me, to die
Would be to go abroad, on a holiday.
And if death should come,
I'd wish I could plan . . . prepare,
As I'd have done,
Looking forward to a happiness
Somewhere, on some cool sand, in the sun,
With sea-sound laden fresh wind for a friend,
Far from the town where weeping has begun.

KOFI ANYIDOHO

Doctrine & Ethics

(for Mallam Femi, Philosophy Teacher)

First   they tried to kill God.

But in order that God might Die
God had to be made a HeMan.
And they gave God a Beard
and a breath of smoking Thunder
and God's face was filled
with glowing Anger.

Their children grew scared
and   retarded from their God.

Then they changed their Mind &
Gave God new attributes of Death:
They painted God White &
Crippled God with a crooked walking stick.

And their children grew listless &
Started throwing stones at their God.

Again they changed their Mind &
Bundled God into a prison house of Words.
And they locked the world out against God.

They accused God of giving birth to Evil.

They charged God with multiple counts
of child neglect. They denied God a hearing
& appointed lifetime interpreters of things God

probably never said   and never did   nor ever will.

And their children grew jealous of attention
And began to quarrel with their fathers' God.

And they changed their Mind
And wrote God up into a Book.
And their God became The Word
And The Word became Their God.

But the World changed   & took The Word along.
And as experience gave birth to new meanings
The Word began to yield multiple images of God.

And a quarrel arose about How their God should Be

Some took God   & filled God with Jealousy.
And their God became Vengeance.
And Vengeance was their God.
And their God became a fearsome WarLord
embarked upon missions of Terror and Horror.

And their children grew scared
And retarded from their God.

Some took God   & filled God with endless
Mercy.
And their God became a clearing house of all
Pardon.

And their children grew reckless
And kicked God in the Face.

And some took God   & made God so Human
God was said to have taken Yusef's wife.
And when God's Child was said to be born
They saddled God's Child with an Ass
and abandoned God's Child among the Sheep.

But their Women took pity on God's Child.
And gave God's Child all their Love.
And vowed as well their Life.

They Tied Down the Women with a Snake.

And when God's Child rebelled
against their nervous conditions
They pinned him down with Words
And they nailed him to a Cross.

And all this Time
God was as patient as Eternity.

(Ragdale House: 31 July 1991)

POLYDAMUS SWALLOWTAIL
BATTUS POLYDAMAS ANTIQUUS

THE CARIBBEAN

CURATED BY ISHION HUTCHINSON

WITH
ANDRE BAGOO, CHRISTIAN CAMPBELL,
KENDEL HIPPOLYTE, NICHOLAS LAUGHLIN,
AND TIPHANIE YANIQUE

RUDDY DAGGERWING
MARPESIA PETREUS

SPHINX JAPIX
UNZELA JAPIX

from In the Marketplace

(Don't mind the noise in the market
only mind the price of the fish)

I

to market to market
to buy a new tongue
home away home away
brigidum brum

the part of me
l share
with you
was not bought
in the marketplace

my father borrowed
pounds sterling
to buy me
a new tongue
at the age of ten
in Canada
one that could speak
in the same breath
the language of Descartes
and Strauss
with the accent
sugar-milled and refined

of a lady
lips soft and pursed

. . .

5

did my father ever guess
that because of his purchase
this tongue was shame
to say *guh mornin?*
the tongue would tell
my eyes to look beyond
a West Indian immigrant
walking on Bloor Street
in Toronto in the '60s

the tidal current
of another tongue
the currency of it
sucked me
under

and my father coloured
colonial and christian
existed somewhere
between somethingness
and nothingness
and somethingmoreness
a putative son
of the enlightenment

and the namesake
of Marcus Garvey

. . .

7

to market to market
to buy a new tongue
home again home again
brigidum bram

I discovered the new market
had no pumpkin cassava peas corn
breadfruit dilly okra grits
this market had no grunts
and goggle-eye fish
and I had no stomach
for trout bass and sweet pears

God! there was too much noise
too many sounds
signals and signs
I could not make out
in the market place

and in my first year
abroad in Toronto
at the age of ten
I could not hear
did not know

when I lost
my accent
and the idiomatic
vernacular swing
of my hips

Iguana

(for A. T.)

My friend from Guyana
was asked in Philadelphia
if she was from "Iguana."

Iguana, which crawls and then
stills, which flicks its tongue at the sun.

In History we learned that Lucayans
ate iguana, that Caribs
(my grandmother's people)
ate Lucayans (the people of Guanahani).
Guiana (the colonial way,
with an *i*, southernmost
of the Caribbean) is iguana; Inagua
(southernmost of The Bahamas,
northernmost of the Caribbean)
is iguana — Inagua, crossroads with Haiti,
Inagua of the salt and flamingos.
The Spanish called it *Heneagua*,
"water is to be found there,"
water, water everywhere.

Guyana (in the language of Arawaks,
Wai Ana, "Land of Many Waters")
is iguana, veins running through land,
grooves between green scales.
My grandmother from Moruga
(southernmost in Trinidad)

knew the names of things.
She rubbed iguana with bird pepper,
she cooked its sweet meat.

The earth is on the back
of an ageless iguana.

We are all from the Land of Iguana,
Hewanorra, Carib name for Saint Lucia.

And all the iguanas scurry away from me.
And all the iguanas are dying.

KAMAU BRATHWAITE, BARBADOS

from Stone

(*for Mikey Smith 1954–1983, stoned to death on Stony Hill, Kingston*)

When the stone fall that morning out of the johncrow sky

it was not dark at first . that opening on to the red sea humming
but something in my mouth like feathers . blue like bubbles
carrying signals & planets & the sliding curve of the
world like a water pic. ture in a raindrop when the pressure. drop

When the stone fall that morning out of the johncrow sky

I couldn't cry out because my mouth was full of beast & plunder
as if I was gnashing badwords among tombstones
as if that road up stony hill . round the bend by the church
yard . on the way to the post office . was a bad bad dream

& the dream was like a snarl of broken copper wire zig zagg.
ing its electric flashes up the hill & splitt. ing spark & flow.
ers high. er up the hill. past the white houses & the ogogs bark.
ing all teeth & fur. nace & my mother like she up . like she up.

like she up. side down up a tree like she was scream.
like she was scream. like she was scream. in no & no.
body i could hear could hear a word i say. in . even though
there were so many poems left & the tape was switched on &

runn. in & runn. in &
the green light was red & they was stannin up there &
evva. where in london & amsterdam & at unesco in paris &
in west berlin & clapp. in & clapp. in & clapp. in &

not a soul on stony hill to even say amen

& yet it was happenin happenin happenin

the fences begin to crack in i skull .
& there was a loud boodooooooooooooooooooooooogs like
guns goin off . them ole time magnums .

or like a fireworks a dreadlocks was on fire .
& the gaps where the river comin down
inna the drei gully where my teeth use to be smilin .
& i tuff gong tongue that use to press against them & parade

pronunciation . now unannounce & like a black wick in i head &
dead .

& it was like a heavy heavy riddim low down in i belly . bleedin dub .
& there was like this heavy heavy black dog thump. in in i chest &

pump. in

murderrrrrrrrrrrrrrrrrrrrrrrrrrrrrrrrrrrrrrrrrrrrrrrrrrrrrrrrrr

& i throat like dem tie. like dem tie. like dem tie a tight tie a.
round it. twist. ing my name quick crick . quick crick .
& a nevva wear neck. tie yet .

& a hear when de big boot kick down i door . stump
in it foot pun a knot in de floor. board .
a window slam shat at de back a mi heart .

de itch & oooze & damp a de yaaad
in my silver tam. bourines closer & closer .
st joseph marching bands crash. ing & closer . &

bom si. cai si. ca boom ship bell . bom si. cai si. ca boom ship bell

& a laughin more blood & spittin out
lawwwwwwwwwwwwwwwwwwwwwwwwwwwwwwwwwwwd

. . .

MARTIN CARTER, GUYANA
Proem

Not, in the saying of you, are you
said. Baffled and like a root
stopped by a stone you turn back questioning
the tree you feed. But what the leaves hear
is not what the roots ask. Inexhaustibly,
being at one time what was to be said
and at another time what has been said
the saying of you remains the living of you
never to be said. But, enduring,
you change with the change that changes
and yet are not of the changing of any of you.
Ever yourself, you are always about
to be yourself in something else ever with me.

FRED D'AGUIAR, GUYANA
Demerara Sugar

In neat sachets where each grain
Flows with crystal clarity in a slalom
Of Swiss blinds ready for my tongue

Sugar cut by hand-swinging cutlass
With half an eye kept on any snake
Wrapping its way around cane fields

Cane pressed for its last ounce of sap
Boiled down to molasses that is cane
Marrow if cane were bones broken

From fields for a bone feast
Demerara whose east coast raised me
From a mere stalk to stand straight

To stand tall no matter what current
Help me find your grain your flow
And Demerara sweeten me

So my art keeps your river's caveat
Your sense of cane fields bathed in sweat

EDWARD BAUGH, JAMAICA
The Carpenter's Complaint

Now you think that is right, sah? Talk the truth.
That man was mi friend. *I* build it, *I*
Build the house that him live in; but now
That him dead, that mawga-foot bwoy, him son,
Come say, him want a nice job for the coffin,
So him give it to *Mister* Belnavis to make —
That big-belly crook who don't know him arse
From a chisel, but because him is big-shot, because
Him make big-shot coffin, fi-him coffin must better
Than mine! Bwoy it hot me, it hot me
For true. Fix we a nex' one, Miss Fergie —
That man coulda knock back him waters, you know sah!
I remember the day in this said-same bar
When him drink Old Brown and Coxs'n into
The ground, then stand up straight as a plumb-line
And keel him felt hat on him head and walk
Home cool, cool, cool. Dem was water-bird, brother!
Funeral? *Me*, sah? That bwoy have to learn
That a man have him pride. But bless mi days!
Good enough to build the house that him live in,
But not good enough to make him coffin!
I woulda do it for nutt'n, for nutt'n! The man
Was mi friend. Damn mawga-foot bwoy.
Is university turn him fool. I tell you,
It burn me, it burn me for true!

Yap

He was remembered
his name becoming a common
noun and verb in regular parlance:

A **yap**

yap \ yap \ *n* **yap•pist** \ ya-pest \ **yap** *vi* **yapped** \ yap-t \
[Youthful innovation Jamaica College] (1974) **1:** HOMOSEXUAL
usually considered obscene **2:** battyman and specialist
in homosexual practices **3:** the scourge of schoolboys
4: their secret fear when clandestine hands cause
self-inflicted sticky orgasms **5:** something no boy admits
he is to other boys (*archaic*)

A gentle boy with a sharp tongue,
he played chess quickly, aggressively
winning with a laugh — played football

in a torn yellow shirt and red shorts;
his father sold radios and calculators
in an air-conditioned appliance store

somewhere downtown and made good money.
They lured him into the piss-stink toilet
flooded with piss and loose shit,

its blue walls scarred with obscenities —
secrets about teachers, yearnings,
hieroglyphics of a twisted culture.

Nuñez, the short Syrian, was the bait
with his tight pants and benign smile —
securing his heterosexual credentials

despite his lisp and delicate eyes.
And they lured Yap into the toilet
where he thought he'd find a friend.

They beat his head till blood
washed the wet cement floor
and his blue shirt turned purple.

This dizzy day of crows circling,
heating to a haze the old cream buildings,
lonely on the feet-worn dust

under the tamarind tree
sat Yap, wiping the blood
from his broken teeth,

tears streaming, frantic to find words
to explain why he wanted to leave
this school and why his shirt was wet

like that. The Citroën sailed in
and stopped. The door opened, swallowed
Yap. The Citroën sailed out.

LORNA GOODISON, JAMAICA

To Us, All Flowers Are Roses

Accompong is Ashanti, root, Nyamekopon.
Appropriate name, Accompong, meaning
warrior or lone one. Accompong,
home to bushmasters, bushmasters being
marooons, maroons dwell in dense places
deep mountainous well sealed
strangers unwelcome. Me No Send You No Come.

I love so the names of this place
how they spring brilliant like "roses"
(to us all flowers are roses), engage you
in flirtation. What is their meaning? Pronunciation?
A strong young breeze that just takes
these names like blossoms and waltzes
them around, turn and wheel them on the tongue.

There are angels in Saint Catherine somewhere.
Arawak is a post office in Saint Ann.
And if the Spaniards hear of this
will they come again in Caravelles
to a post office (in suits of mail)
to inquire after any remaining Arawaks?
Nice people, so gentle, peaceful, and hospitable.

There is everywhere here.
There is Alps and Lapland and Berlin.
Armagh, Carrick Fergus, Malvern
Rhine and Calabar, Askenish
where freed slaves went to claim

what was left of the Africa within
staging secret woodland ceremonies.

Such ceremonies! such dancing, ai Kumina!
drum sound at Barking Lodge where we hear
a cargo of slaves landed free, because
somebody signed a paper even as they
rode as cargo shackled on the high seas.
So they landed here, were unchained, went free.
So in some places there is almost pure Africa.

Some of it is lost, though, swept away forever,
maybe at Lethe in Hanover, Lethe springs
from the Greek, a river which is the river
of Oblivion. There is Mount Peace here
and Tranquility and Content. May Pen,
Dundee Pen, Bamboo Pen and for me,
Faith's Pen, therefore will I write.

There is Blackness here which is sugar land
and they say is named for the ebony of the soil.
At a wedding there once the groom wore cobalt blue
and young bride, cloud white, at Blackness.
But there is blood, red blood in the fields
of our lives, blood the bright banner flowing
over the order of cane and our history.

The Hope River in hot times goes under,
but pulses underground strong enough to rise
again and swell to new deep, when the May rains
fall for certain. There was a surfeit once

of Swine in Fat Hog quarter and somehow
Chateau Vert slipped on the Twi of our tongue
and fell to rise up again as "Shotover."

They hung Paul Bogle's body at sea
so there is blood too in the sea, especially
at Bloody Bay where they punctured balloons
of great grey whales. There is Egypt here
at Catadupa, a name they spoke first softly
to the white falling cataracts of the Nile.
There is Amity and Friendship and Harmony Hall.

Stonehenge . . . Sevens, Duppy Gate, Wait a Bit,
Wild Horses, Tan and See, Time and Patience,
Unity. It is Holy here, Mount Moses
dew falls on Mount Nebo, south of Jordan,
Mount Nebo, rises here too hola Mount Zion high.
Paradise is found here, from Pisgah we look out
and Wait a Bit, Wild Horses, Tan and See, Time and Patience, Unity.

For the wounded a Doctor's Cave
and at Phoenix Park from Burnt Ground new rising.
Good Hope, the mornings dawn crystalline
at Cape Clear. It is good for brethren
and sistren to dwell together in Unity
on Mount Pleasant. Doctor Breezes issue from the side
of the sea across parishes named for saints.

Rivers can be tied together in eights.
Mountains are Lapis Lazuli or Sapphire,
impossibly blue and rivers wag their waters

or flow Black or White or of Milk.
And the waters of the Fish River do contain
and will yield up good eating fish. O heart
when some nights you cannot sleep,

for wondering why you have been charged
to keep some things of which you cannot speak,
think what release will mean, when your name
is changed to Tranquility. I was born at Lineen —
Jubilee! — on the anniversary of Emancipation Day.
I recite these names in a rosary, speak them
when I pray, for Heartease, my Mecca, aye Jamaica.

SHARA MCCALLUM, JAMAICA
What the Oracle Said

You will leave your home:
nothing will hold you.
You will wear dresses of gold; skins
of silver, copper, and bronze.
The sky above you will shift in meaning
each time you think you understand.
You will spend a lifetime chipping away layers
of flesh. The shadow of your scales
will always remain. You will be marked
by sulphur and salt.
You will bathe endlessly in clear streams and fail
to rid yourself of that scent.
Your feet will never be your own.
Stone will be your path.
Storms will follow in your wake,
destroying all those who take you in.
You will desert your children
kill your lovers and devour their flesh.
You will love no one
but the wind and ache of your bones.
Neither will love you in return.
With age, your hair will grow matted and dull,
your skin will gape and hang in long folds,
your eyes will cease to shine.
But nothing will be enough.
The sea will never take you back.

CLAUDE MCKAY, JAMAICA

If We Must Die

If we must die, let it not be like hogs
Hunted and penned in an inglorious spot,
While round us bark the mad and hungry dogs,
Making their mock at our accursèd lot.
If we must die, O, let us nobly die,
So that our precious blood may not be shed
In vain; then even the monsters we defy
Shall be constrained to honor us though dead!
O kinsmen! we must meet the common foe!
Though far outnumbered let us show us brave,
And for their thousand blows deal one death-blow!
What though before us lies the open grave?
Like men we'll face the murderous, cowardly pack,
Pressed to the wall, dying, but fighting back!

ANTHONY MCNEILL, JAMAICA
Hello Ungod

Ungod my lungs blacken
the cities have fallen
the easy prescriptions
have drilled final holes in my cells
Ungod my head sieves in the wind
Ungod I am sterile
Ungod it appears
I am dying
Ungod I am scared
Ungod can you hear me
Ungod I am testing for levels
Ungod testing 1 2 3
Ungod are you evil
Ungod I can't hear you
Ungod I am trying
Ungod I can't reach you
Ungod my lungs blacken
the cities have fallen
head sieves in the wind

Ungod disconnecting.

KEI MILLER, JAMAICA
Some Definitions for Light (I)

— [etymology] photo, root word for light, hence photology — the
study of light. Photometer — the measurement of light.
Photophilia, the love of light; the photophilic are drawn
helpless, like sunflowers whose round faces travel across the day
like the hand of a clock, like Agatha who insisted on dying even
though she was well. Photomania, an obsession with light — in
1974 a man was found sweating in his small room, surrounded
by a congregation of lamps, 137 bulbs burning, even during the
day he was trying to create. Photophobia, the fear of light.
Photophobics hide in shadows; their eyes hurt. The
photophobic cannot read this; they are at risk of going blind.
Blindness could be called photominimus or photomaximus. It
is, at once, the absence and the great excess of light — the belly
of a cave and its opening. Photogenic — concerning the basic
helix strands of light, and also the ability to birth light. A
photographer is one who writes about it; a photograph is
writing composed of it — of brilliant, brilliant light. Look. Look
closely — this is a photograph.

DENNIS SCOTT, JAMAICA
Epitaph

They hanged him on a clement morning, swung
between the falling sunlight and the women's
breathing, like a black apostrophe to pain.
All morning while the children hushed
their hopscotch joy and the cane kept growing
he hung there sweet and low.
                    At least that's how
they tell it. It was long ago
and what can we recall of a dead slave or two
except that when we punctuate our island tale
they swing like sighs across the brutal
sentences, and anger pauses
till they pass away.

OLIVE SENIOR, JAMAICA
Peppercorn

Torn from the vine in a place of moist
heat and shade where I was growing,
skin once plump and reddish, glowing.
Suddenly, a job lot. Indiscriminately
thrown in, we are jumbled, shaken up,
rolled together, little knowing our fate
or destination, till black and shriveled
by the sun, looking all alike now, we are
tumbled into hold of a ship for forty days
and forty nights (we guess — for black
is the fenestration).

Disgorged, spilled out, shell-shocked
I come parched and dried, my head
emptied, till shock-still I come to rest,
shelled out, buck naked. In the mad
ensuing scramble, who will come
        who will come sample me,
view me, choose me, sort me out
for grade and quality, drive me home
to crush me, use me? Know that alone
I'm of little value, like a peppercorn
rental. All together, we can pepper
your arse with shot.

Over time, despite our treatment,
you'll see, survivors stay pungent
and hot. You can beat me senseless,
grind me down, crush me to bits, to

powder. You can never lose my bite
on your tongue, my hold on your senses:
forever I'll linger and cling.

In your mad scramble to possess,
devour me, remember, if you'd only
allow me to do a striptease, slow, peel off
my black skin, you'd be pleased —
or shocked — to discover: I'm white below.

TANYA SHIRLEY, JAMAICA

A West Indian Poem

It is not the first time our house
has killed a bird

but that red smeared
like shield and omen

sucked up all the sun, the breeze, the slopes,
the trees, the colour.

I thought of the woman rising from her evening prayers
shot dead in her house last night,

of impending elections,
of the faces, each week more and more, in the *Gleaner*'s obituary,

I thought of my grandmother sitting with the older spirits
begging pardon for how we have wasted

the blood they fought to keep,
the blood below the sea, the cotton, the sugar, the whip.

Perhaps tonight when the dream stealers
are on the prowl,

a dead bird's dried blood will remind them of God
and we shall be passed over.

Behind God Back

You come from a two-be-three island
hard like rock
black you have another handicap
and you come from Long Ground
way behind God back.

They taught you like a fool
never told you miles of cotton
went to Liverpool
to line the Bank of England
from Long Ground behind God back
he shoulda turned round
and catch the thieves white-handed
white and black

They took you for an imbecile
never told you Montserrat tobacco
made W. D. and H. O. Wills
rich testators of Bristol University
lighting their names on the crest of history
with Long Ground tobacco
bought behind God back

Never told you how your mother strong
to carry buckra cotton
and his seed
fertile like Long Ground soil
strong to carry bales of history
and buckra deeds heavy like a sack
of cotton picked behind God back

People in the town
didn't know off-white and brown were black
until they went to England
Powell vote to pack them back
rejected like stained cotton
didn't know when God turned round
his smile like a rainbow
lit Long Ground with hope
and cotton children weave boot strap
to pull themselves up
from behind God back

Night Vision

I

It's hard to see anything without history.
Days leave their residue, a film over the eyes,
far more the centuries. We see by memory
and the memories of generations become cataracts
occluding the child-clear visioning of Eden.
Because we see with history,
it is difficult to see through it. And yet we must
or we become it, become nothing else but history.

2

But how to see, yet see beyond:
three caravels whose keels severed the horizon line between the worlds,
Columbus's abscessive dreams rupturing, blood on the white sand of centuries
clotting into countries of a new map of the world;
to see beyond:
canoe-eyed warriors women children beautiful as pottery,
their red-earth bodies pitted from insidious arrows of plague,
their glazing eyes holding the dimming stare of their last zemis;
how to see:
the desperate indentured servants, scarecrow tobacco farmers
who'd fled from hungering Ireland, the hardening boundaries of England,
chewed to white trash in the grinding maws of sugar factories;
beyond:
millions of Africans contorted into writings of black coral on the sea-floor,

and the survivors living the other death, from the first lash of sunlight
till the cool, blessed dark dried out the whip and cutlass
while they unburied, nightly, the still-warm, holy, undying dream.
How
to see yet see beyond?

3

To see through history, you have to journey back
not so much into time as into self.
Reading, late night, the pages furl past like waves
and you are following the compass point of the imagination.
Scanning centuries, you scry for traces, the glyphs of who you were.
On such journeys, you may sail the coast of a whole era
and not once make landfall. But sometimes, following true north,
you leave the sea, walk inland, then further inland, deep
to the interior of one moment:
Cape Coast. Outside a barracoon. John Newton and an African slaver
haggle over the bowed head of a man kneeling between them.
They do not know him or the trade would end.
But why your feet are stiffening to stone, your mind to ice
as the third man looks up, you know.
The jerk of recognition is a body blow. It doubles you.
And then your feet are raging, your arms are sorrowing out
toward yourself, toward
                              the shock as, eye for eye,
you are stood stock-still by the strange familiar looks of the two men.
Now eye to eye, you recognize
again, and then again, your face.
Which self do you save?

On the journeys inland, you retrace
the inner lineaments of ancestry.
Late night. You close the book
of history.

4

Let them go, gently. All of them: Columbus and his frightened crew of felons;
the Carib warriors of Sauteurs Cliff who leaped to meet themselves; Hawkins,
d'Esnambuc, the swarm of barracuda privateers; Makandal, Bussa, and all of the
enslaved who never became slaves; the great house masters, the rebels, the infor-
mants, the runaways, the broken at the wheel, the sad infanticidal mothers . . .
Let them all rest.
Let them fall into a welcoming sunlit water to a deep, final settling.
Now the loud rodomontade and dazzlingblind dingolay of history's carnival parade
stutters toward silence, dims to a dwindled glimpse
of you closing a book in the frame of a lit window.
Even that will go.
The window blind will draw down like an eyelid closing, leaving
your self in the illumination that discovers you
only in darkness.

JANE KING, SAINT LUCIA
Saint Joseph at the Music School

The wind sussurating the shak-shak trees
almost drowning the sounds of the sea
and the children performing for teachers
in the building behind me.
My small son suffers his lesson
silently.

The perfect turquoise of the bay
a green arm of the harbour with a frilled cuff
where the surf breaks on Tapion rock.

The soothing breeze that shakes the trees
blowing gently round my knees,
grapefruit shine yellow in dark leaves —
it is enough.

It has to be enough.

Yesterday
we heard the archbishop say
Saint Joseph is the patron
of a happy death.

DEREK WALCOTT, SAINT LUCIA
from The Schooner *Flight*

1 Adios, Carenage

In idle August, while the sea soft,
and leaves of brown islands stick to the rim
of this Caribbean, I blow out the light
by the dreamless face of Maria Concepcion
to ship as a seaman on the schooner *Flight*.
Out in the yard turning gray in the dawn,
I stood like a stone and nothing else move
but the cold sea rippling like galvanize
and the nail holes of stars in the sky roof,
till a wind start to interfere with the trees.
I pass me dry neighbor sweeping she yard
as I went downhill, and I nearly said:
"Sweep soft, you witch, 'cause she don't sleep hard,"
but the bitch look through me like I was dead.
A route taxi pull up, park-lights still on.
The driver size up my bags with a grin:
"This time, Shabine, like you really gone!"
I ain't answer the ass, I simply pile in
the back seat and watch the sky burn
above Laventille pink as the gown
in which the woman I left was sleeping,
and I look in the rearview and see a man
exactly like me, and the man was weeping
for the houses, the streets, that whole fucking island.

Christ have mercy on all sleeping things!
From that dog rotting down Wrightson Road
to when I was a dog on these streets;

if loving these islands must be my load,
out of corruption my soul takes wings.
But they had started to poison my soul
with their big house, big car, big-time bohbohl,
coolie, nigger, Syrian, and French Creole,
so I leave it for them and their carnival —
I taking a sea bath, I gone down the road.
I know these islands from Monos to Nassau,
a rusty head sailor with sea-green eyes
that they nickname Shabine, the patois for
any red nigger, and I, Shabine, saw
when these slums of empire was paradise.
I'm just a red nigger who love the sea,
I had a sound colonial education,
I have Dutch, nigger, and English in me,
and either I'm nobody, or I'm a nation.

But Maria Concepcion was all my thought
watching the sea heaving up and down
as the port side of dories, schooners, and yachts
was painted afresh by the strokes of the sun
signing her name with every reflection;
I knew when dark-haired evening put on
her bright silk at sunset, and, folding the sea,
sidled under the sheet with her starry laugh,
that there'd be no rest, there'd be no forgetting.
Is like telling mourners round the graveside
about resurrection, they want the dead back,
so I smile to myself as the bow rope untied
and the *Flight* swing seaward: "Is no use repeating
that the sea have more fish. I ain't want her

dressed in the sexless light of a seraph,
I want those round brown eyes like a marmoset, and
till the day when I can lean back and laugh,
those claws that tickled my back on sweating
Sunday afternoons, like a crab on wet sand."
As I worked, watching the rotting waves come
past the bow that scissor the sea like silk,
I swear to you all, by my mother's milk,
by the stars that shall fly from tonight's furnace,
that I loved them, my children, my wife, my home;
I loved them as poets love the poetry
that kills them, as drowned sailors the sea.

You ever look up from some lonely beach
and see a far schooner? Well, when I write
this poem, each phrase go be soaked in salt;
I go draw and knot every line as tight
as ropes in this rigging; in simple speech
my common language go be the wind,
my pages the sails of the schooner *Flight*.
But let me tell you how this business begin.

SHAKE KEANE, SAINT VINCENT AND THE GRENADINES
from Thirteen Studies in Home Economics

Lesson Five: Per Capita Per Annum

Number of people under review —
  91000. Percentage of invisible fathers
    or mothers of haphazard status —
      79 (or more). Number of people
        who pay taxes — too many
          or too few. Number of people
            who starve; number of people who
              eat; number of people
                who eat people who starve . . .
                  Number of humans, hybrids,
                    hermaphrodites,
                      hominids . . .

hogsheads of hate

still wait to be opened

in the headquarters of the hungry

Number of large heads, spring beds
  large bellies, distended guts, percentage
    of placentas per square-inch of a
      school-yard; estimate of prostitutes
        per public-centimeter of a cradle.
          Number of beggars, wooden legs,
            scrunters, hunters, highest-
              common-factor of broken skulls
                per milli-litre of strong rum;
                  of broken hearts per man-hour
                    of gossip, percentage of
                      sheep per driver . . .

in heaven in 1976
there were thousands of suicides
who giggled

Estimates of imports in proportion to bans
  on imports; gross shipping in proportion
    to fishing boats per hundred; cares
      in proportion to arise-holes of population;
        makes of cars, number of types
          of number-plates of cars.
            Visitors who cannot relate to home,
              divided by tourist who cannot
              pay
                to leave home.
                  Vice against vaccinations,
                    lawyers against builders,
                      dreams
                        against people
                          who cannot sleep . . .

then there was feasting
in the streets of Kush
when the last slave
returned healthy with treasure
from Taiwan

Percentage of decibels to blossoms;
  number of quiet people, fearless people;
    number of people decently assaulted
      by other people; square-roots of gardens
        inhabited by paranoid mongrels,
          percentage of poems
            damaged in transport,

act of love and labour
accurately recognizable
as pleasure . . .

everyone remembers
not a single song
of the Callinagos

Graphs to indicate the upward and downward
  curve of arrowroot; segments
    of social circles removed by surgery.
      Emergency graves for the heads
        of stolen cattle.
          Straw hats and straw mats;
            hundreds of people
              with rock-faces fishing for status;
                nine people fishing
                  with rods on rocks
                    with lanterns
                      ole mas' faces
                        lights without luster
                          crabs . . .

but I could name you
by name
the first Spaniard
who vomited into his guitar

182000 noseholes under review.
  Hunters and scrunters too many or
    too few. Petites of baby-killing semen;
      popcorn; popsicles
        with number-plates;

the downward curve of pigeon-peas,
poems, cognition and recognition
that died thrashing
in an abandoned
ambulance . . .

when I was a child
you could buy Aztec soulfood
outside the temple of Nineveh

Numbers of numbers —
bers, bers, blurs, — NUMB, — oh so numb . . .
Exodus, Leviticus, numbers,
levies, lies, lassitudes . . .

Numberless people under review.
Number of THEM — 91000.
Number of US — 91000.
Till death
give us a head-start —
per capita
per annum
every year
HERE . . .

during
next lesson
Lesson Six
those who so wish
will be taught how to count

(Saint Vincent: 21 June 1975)

JAMES CHRISTOPHER ABOUD, TRINIDAD AND TOBAGO

Wind, Water, Fire, Men

Lagahoo takes his shape from the wind;
Wind has no shape, but
Gives shape to the sails of the men's boats
        and the shape of ocean hedges.
Without the shape of things to press against,
        wind has no shape,
And yet Lagahoo presses against all things
And all things against him,
And each and each are different.

Lagahoo takes his shape from the fire;
Fire has no shape
Except the shape of those it makes its servants.
Without servants, fire cannot be,
        yet Lagahoo has no master.

The shape of water is not caused by water,
But by the palms of Lagahoo's hands and his beaches.
Water tumbles through the ages
Much as it tumbles through the rocks,
Without hindrance.
Without Lagahoo, water has no shape,
But Lagahoo takes his shape from the water.

The shape of the man is the shape of darkness
But the man's senses are full of light,
And Lagahoo takes his shape also from the men
And their senses.

The day does not see the night,
Nor the sun the moon.
The word does not become the idea
Nor do the birds join the conversation of whales.

And yet in the senses of men,
The day sees the night
The sun sees the moon
The word embraces the idea:

And so Lagahoo came to touch his nature,
And know its shape.

DIONNE BRAND, TRINIDAD AND TOBAGO
from Land to Light On

XII

Out of them. To where? As if I wasn't them.
To this I suppose. The choices fallen into
and unmade. Out of them. Out of shape
and glimmer and into hissing prose. What
could it mean, all that ocean, all that bush,
all that room, all that hemmed and sweet light.
Don't be mistaken, the whole exercise was
for escaping, the body cut so, the tongue cut
so, the drape of the head and the complications
boiling to their acid verbs. This pine was waiting,
this road already travelled, this sea in the back
of my head roiling its particular wrecks
and like escaping one doesn't look too close
at landing, any desert is lush, sand blooms,
any grit in the mouth is peace, the mechanics
of a hummingbird less blazing than the whirr,
all at once calligraphy and spun prism, this new
landfall when snows come and go and come again,
this landfall happened at your exact flooding and
even though you had a mind, well, landing . . .
it doesn't count on flesh or memory, or any purposes

VAHNI CAPILDEO, TRINIDAD AND TOBAGO
from Time is an Unkind Dancer

Light and Dark

"On a planet where the sun rises
  just once every six months,
  light, in its slightest manifestation,
  will be worshipped — will it not?

"The tiniest sequin reflector,
  minute pinhead matchsticks,
  the devices, the receptacles,
  for any kind of flame —
  they would be precious, shy, expensive.
  Birthday lamps would be few
  but large, and unspeakably gorgeous.
  The words of love, the name of friendship,
  all would be gifts of light — ?"

"No.

"Total and absolute is the love
  of darkness. Light achieves
  no more than clarity — not even;
  it blurs, without solving.

"With what passionate serenity
  the adherents of dark
  cut that world's bare wind with their faces!
  Their work is like dancing.
  It is the stretch when the tear has healed,
  dark, the home after time,

it is the calm where monsters are safe
to move one limb every million years
to finish their embrace."

Though,
as a matter of fact, on that planet
the sun is taboo. The trade
in contraband lamps,
re-jigged leaking batteries,
black-market torches,
all sorts, is exorbitant.
Matches are cruelly taxed.
The level of theft is high.
Pearl-finish cigarette lighters
are built with a flick-knife component.
The keeping of pets is forbidden.
The hoarding of tallow is rife.

Therefore
the second speaker was punished
in the sense saturation chamber.
Brilliance on brilliance destroyed her
as, laid out like a starfish,
she smiled from her vanishing eyepoints
as if their visions were reconciled.

MAHADAI DAS, TRINIDAD AND TOBAGO

They Came in Ships

They came in ships
  From far across the seas
    Britain, colonising the East in India
      Transporting her chains from Chota Nagpur and the Ganges plain.
     Westwards came the *Whitby*
    Like the *Hesperus*
   Alike the island-bound *Fatel Rozack.*

     Wooden missions of imperialist design.
     Human victims of her Majesty's victory.

      They came in fleets of ships.
      They came in droves
      Like cattle.
      Brown like cattle,
      Eyes limpid, like cattle.

      Some came with dreams of milk and honey riches.
      Others came, fleeing famine
      And death,
      All alike, they came —
      The dancing girls,
      Rajput soldiers — tall and proud
      Escaping the penalty of their pride.
      The stolen wives — afraid and despondent.
      All alike,
      Crossing dark waters.
      Brahmin and Chamar alike.
      They came
     At least with hope in their heart.
     On the platter of the plantocracy
    They were offered disease and death.

     I saw them dying at the street-corners
     Alone and hungry, they died
     Starving for the want of a crumb of British bread
    And the touch of a healing hand.

     Today, I remember my forefather's gaunt gaze.
     My mind's eye sweeps over my children of yesterday
     My children of tomorrow.
    The piracy of innocence.
    The loss of light in their eyes.

    I stand between posterity's horizon
   And her history.
I, alone today, am alive,
Seeing beyond, looking ahead.

I do not forget the past that has moulded the present.
The present is a caterer for the future.
I remember logies
Barrackroom ranges
Nigga-yards.
My grandmother worked in the field.
Honourable mention.

Creole gang, child labour —
Second prize.
I remember Lallabhagie.
Can I forget how Enmore rose in arms
For the children of Leonora?

Remember one-third quota
Coolie woman.
Was your blood spilled so that I might reject my history?
Forget tears in shadow — paddy leaves.

Here, at the edge of the horizon
I hear voices crying in the wind.
Cuffy shouting — Remember 1763.
John Smith — At least, if I am a man of God,
Let me join forces with black suffering.
Akkarra — I too had a vision
Before I lost it.
Atta — in the beginning, I was with the struggle.
And Des Voeux cried
I wrote the Queen a letter
For the whimpering of the coolies
In their logies would not let me rest.

Beaumont — Had the law been in my hands.
And the cry of the coolies
Echoed around the land.
They came in droves
At the door of his office
Beseeching him to ease the yoke off their burden.
And Crosby struck in rage
Against the planters
In vain
He was stripped naked of his rights
And the cry of the coolies continued.

The Commissioners came
Capital spectacles with British frames
Consulting managers
About the cost of immigration.
They forgot the purpose of their coming.
The commissioners left,
Fifty-dollar bounty remained.
Dreams of a cow and endless calves
And endless reality, in chains.

Ode to My Unknown Great-Great-Grandmother

I heard you were the first
to belong nowhere.
Born on the wide Kala Pani
between Calcutta and Port-of-Spain
on a ship unknown.

Your parents, indentured labourers,
coolies from India,
lost their dreams of returning home
in canefields of Caroni.

But you grew and you spoke
not Sanskrit or Urdu pure,
but broken Bhojpuri Hindi.
You prayed to Shiva
dancing on Gangetic Plains
you never saw.

Your eyes were the first to embrace
El Toucuche and Ciero Del Aripo.
You were the first to season
your curry mango with bandhania,
wild coriander, shadon beni
instead of true dhania
coriander from India.
Your bare feet were the first to claim
dirt paths from Cedros to Las Cuevas.

I have tried to reincarnate
you in my womb,
but I have failed.
My eyes are the last to gaze
upon the Scarlet Ibis
roosting in the Caroni Swamp.

My feet are the last to walk
the forests of Mathura.
My blood the last to make
red tikkaa on the forehead
of La Trinity.
My ashes are the last to belong somewhere.

MERVYN MORRIS, TRINIDAD AND TOBAGO

Peelin Orange

Dem use to seh
yu peel a orange
perfec
an yu get new clothes

But when mi father try
fi teach mi
slide de knife
up to de safeguard thumb

I move de weapon like
a saw inna mi han
an de dyamn rind
break

An if yu have de time
yu can come see mi
in mi ole clothes
peelin

M. NOURBESE PHILIP, TRINIDAD AND TOBAGO

Discourse on the Logic of Language

English
is my mother tongue.
A mother tongue is not
not a foreign lan lan lang
language
l/anguish
  anguish
— a foreign anguish.

English is
my father tongue.
A father tongue is
a foreign language,
therefore English is
a foreign language
not a mother tongue.

What is my mother
tongue
my mammy tongue
my mummy tongue
my momsy tongue
my modder tongue
my ma tongue?

I have no mother
tongue
no mother to tongue

WHEN IT WAS BORN, THE MOTHER HELD HER NEWBORN CHILD CLOSE: SHE BEGAN THEN TO LICK IT ALL OVER. THE CHILD WHIMPERED A LITTLE, BUT AS THE MOTHER'S TONGUE MOVED FASTER AND STRONGER OVER ITS BODY, IT GREW SILENT — THE MOTHER TURNING IT THIS WAY AND THAT UNDER HER TONGUE, UNTIL SHE HAD TONGUED IT CLEAN OF THE CREAMY WHITE SUBSTANCE COVERING ITS BODY.

EDICT I

*Every owner of slaves
shall, whenever possible,
ensure that his slaves
belong to as many ethno-
linguistic groups as
possible. If they can-
not speak to each other,
they cannot then foment
rebellion and revolution.*

no tongue to mother
to mother
tongue
me

I must therefore be tongue
dumb
dumb-tongued
dub-tongued
damn dumb
tongue

Those parts of the brain chiefly responsible for speech are named
after two learned nineteenth century doctors, the eponymous
Doctors Wernicke and Broca respectively.

Dr. Broca believed the size of the brain determined intelligence;
he devoted much of his time to 'proving' that white males of the
Caucasian race had larger brains than, and were therefore superior
to, women, Blacks, and other peoples of colour.

Understanding and recognition of the spoken word takes place
in Wernicke's area — the left temporal lobe, situated next to the
auditory cortex; from there relevant information passes to Broca's
area — situated in the left frontal cortex — which then forms the
response and passes it on to the motor cortex. The motor cortex
controls the muscles of speech.

THE MOTHER THEN PUT HER FINGERS INTO HER CHILD'S MOUTH — GENTLY FORCING IT OPEN; SHE TOUCHES HER TONGUE TO THE CHILD'S TONGUE, AND HOLDING THE TINY MOUTH OPEN, SHE BLOWS INTO IT — HARD. SHE WAS BLOWING WORDS — HER WORDS, HER MOTHER'S WORDS, THOSE OF HER MOTHER'S MOTHER, AND ALL THEIR MOTHERS BEFORE — INTO HER DAUGHTER'S MOUTH.

but I have
a dumb tongue
tongue dumb
father tongue
and english is
my mother tongue
is
my father tongue
is a foreign lan lan lang
language
l/anguish
  anguish
a foreign anguish
is english —
another tongue
my mother
    mammy
    mummy
    moder
    mater
    macer
    moder
tongue
mothertongue

tongue mother
tongue me
mothertongue me
mother me
touch me
with the tongue of your
lan lan lang

EDICT II

Every slave caught speaking his native language shall be severely punished. Where necessary, removal of the tongue is recommended. The offending organ, when removed, should be hung on high in a central place, so that all may see and tremble.

language
l/anguish
  anguish
english
is a foreign anguish

A tapering, blunt-tipped, muscular, soft and fleshy organ describes
(a) the penis.
(b) the tongue.
(c) neither of the above.
(d) both of the above.

In man the tongue is
(a) the principal organ of taste.
(b) the principal organ of articulate speech.
(c) the principal organ of oppression and
    exploitation.
(d) all of the above.

The tongue
(a) is an interwoven bundle of striated muscle running in three planes.
(b) is fixed to the jawbone.
(c) has an outer covering of a mucous membrane covered with papillae.
(d) contains ten thousand taste buds, none of which is sensitive to the taste of foreign words.

Air is forced out of the lungs up the throat to the larynx where it causes the vocal cords to vibrate and create sound. The metamorphosis from sound to intelligible word requires

(a) the lip, tongue and jaw all working together.

(b) a mother tongue.

(c) the overseer's whip.

(d) all of the above or none.

JENNIFER RAHIM, TRINIDAD AND TOBAGO
Haiti

For the earth has spoken,
to you, her magma Creole.

Full-throated syllables, up-
rising from deep down,

an honest elocution —
rudimentary sound: guttural

nouns, forthright, strong,
the rumbled conviction of verbs

unfettered by reticence
as the first poetry of creation.

A secret has passed between you
so wonderfully terrible,

it laid your cities prostrate,
raptured your citizenry.

Now, we look to your remnant
courtesy cable TV

and garble theories thinking
ourselves saved.

Only the wise among us pin
our ears to the ground,

listening in hope of catching
even a half syllable

of the language forming
like a new world on your tongue.

MARVIN E. WILLIAMS, THE VIRGIN ISLANDS
Noontide, Fort Christian

A shrieking seagull catapults
from sun's niggering rays, his wings slapping
winds which swat the slack flaps
of sailboats huddled, besieged seadogs,
groggy in this hurricane portal.

The epileptic noontime froths at the mouth
of the channel, hawking, spitting its ague
halfway up the thick Fort Christian walls,
walls rejuvenated in ripe-wound red
for the tourist's bandaged dollar.

Cannons preside above the spastic waves,
miming eurekas for eardrums timbred by
Cortez's thunder. Their Blue Beardian eyes dim
from wildfire into hearth for those visitors
wondering at this
relic of empire in black gestation.

With maps ushering them down hallways
metabolized in their blood,
they photograph the Rustoleumed cages
whose clangs clutch the slave woman's
conflagration,
the bones of her cohorts,
the bones of her cutthroats,
the ashen communion of ghosts.

HABIB TIWONI, THE VIRGIN ISLANDS
'Pon Top Bluebeard Castle Hill

In that jungled hill
lies the ruins of adolescence
(in the grassland of time)
the old twisted and burnt
cruder bag whose smoke
sucked bees from their
honey combs

Ducking there in our green garden
from Jack Spania's lancin' hair
were peppercinnamons, male papayas,
wild tamarind and casha that
tore up the skin like scratches
on a lover's back

But (in the jungle I was king
to me the burds came daily to sing)

Kilinke birds trottin' across the road
disappearing into the white maran bush
as we pitched barrages of curved stones
into the pigeon berry and fiddlewood trees

There our backs bristled with
broom palms, frangipani, jackocalalu,
almonds, growing sweet basil and poinsettia

And (in the jungle I was king
to me the burds came daily to sing)
until the senses awoke one day
and saw their selfish signs
"no trespassing."

SOUTH AFRICA

CURATED BY RUSTUM KOZAIN

GAUDY COMMODORE
PRECIS OCTAVIA

ARTHUR NORTJE
Native's Letter

Habitable planets are unknown or too
far away from us to be
of consequence. To be of
value to his homeland must the wanderer
not weep by northern waters, but love
his own bitter clay
roaming through the hard cities, tough
himself as coffin nails.

Harping on the nettles of his melancholy,
keening on the blue strings of the blood,
he will delve into mythologies perhaps
call up spirits through the night,

or carry memories apocryphal
of Tshaka, Hendrik, Witbooi, Adam Kok,
of the Xhosa nation's dream
as he moonlights in another country:

but he shall also have
cycles of history
outnumbering the guns of supremacy.

Now and whenever he arrives
extending feelers into foreign scenes
exploring times and lives,
equally may he stand and laugh,
explode with a paper bag of poems,
burst upon a million televisions

with a face as in a Karsh photograph,
slave voluntarily in some siberia
to earn the salt of victory.

Darksome, whoever dies
in the malaise of my dear land
remember me at swim,
the moving waters spilling through my eyes:
and let no amnesia
attack at fire hour:
for some of us must storm the castles
some define the happening.

(Toronto: May 1970)

CHRIS VAN WYK

In Detention

He fell from the ninth floor
He hanged himself
He slipped on a piece of soap while washing
He hanged himself
He slipped on a piece of soap while washing
He fell from the ninth floor
He hanged himself while washing
He slipped from the ninth floor
He hung from the ninth floor
He slipped on the ninth floor while washing
He fell from a piece of soap while slipping
He hung from the ninth floor
He washed from the ninth floor while slipping
He hung from a piece of soap while washing.

PETER HORN
from "The Plumstead Elegies"

The Fourth Elegy

Men of this town, why are we winter sad?
Have we not, like migrating birds,
communicated our intention? In the lateness of this hour
are we not prepared to take wing?
To rise from the stagnant pools of white feathers?
Do we not scent, long before we arrive, the rain-drenched
flowering of our destination? What are riot vans
and squad cars against our purpose?

The drink is bitter, if we have to sip the dregs.
But hunger and thirst are not preordained: We've got heads.
Let's use them! Let us imagine chaos,
confusion, the end of law and order,
of 180 days detention, of bannings and censorship.
Just the thought will upset a lot of people
and will give them ulcers.

To think that even these towns will come to an end,
like others before, like Babylon the Whore,
like Sodom and Ghomorrha.
Remember, they were towns just like our towns:
somewhat smaller than Johannesburg and Cape Town,
but the stench of poverty and the smell of exploitation
was pungent in the morning and sickening in the evening,
and the fight for a penny was waged in the streets and markets
with the same fierceness as in Adderley Street.

We can imagine the exhilarating chaos when one day
the water supply fails, and the next the electricity
goes dead in Constantia; the robots turn blind
during peak hour traffic. Because life will go on,
naturally, between
gun shots, and people will drink beer and brandy,
and confide their astonishment to their
no longer privileged friends
about how it could have happened at all when the army
was so well organized and the police force so strong,
and BOSS must have been sleeping.

And it will be irritating, if you are suddenly no longer allowed to say
just what you like, I mean common phrases like "Voertsêk,
Kaffir!"
you could even get jailed for that.
And the consternation of the parents
if Rondebosch High became fully integrated,
if no merciful law stood between them and their
liberal statements.
And worse things can happen: justice, the watchdog of
earthly possessions,
might no longer protect the haves with democratic impartiality:
the rich might be punished more harshly than the poor.
We can imagine how the sufferers confront their tormentors,
last survivors in front of those that destined them to die,
and demand that they be punished for legal acts
like electrocuting witnesses, whipping enemies of the state,
hanging a labourer by his feet from a tree,
pouring boiling water in his mouth
when he said that he was thirsty,
and flogging him to death, because he was "cheeky."

And they, no longer men of great and important deeds,
no longer violent actors, as we know them
from fairy tales, myths and history books,
no longer terrifying blond beasts, colonels, generals,
will confess uniform cruelties, repeated a thousand times,
committed a short time ago, now, while we are living.

Incredible things could happen! The mind boggles to contemplate
that workers, actual workers, could take over factories,
and organize work for the benefit of workers,
the owners suddenly freed from their tremendous
responsibility to the nation, jobless, penniless,
reduced to beg, as they have learnt no trade.

Nostalgia is sure to set in amongst the poverty-stricken rich,
sighs, how the times have changed,
how everything was better, when you still could make a profit
importing witless mine boys from another country,
when the native knew his place and was respectful.
Oh yes, we can imagine it, this is how it will be.

JEREMY CRONIN
[To learn how to speak]

To learn how to speak
With the voices of this land,
To parse the speech in its rivers,
To catch in the inarticulate grunt,
Stammer, call, cry, babble, tongue's knot
A sense of the stoneness of these stones
From which all words are cut.
To trace with the tongue wagon-trails
Saying the suffix of their aches in -kuil, -pan, -fontein,
In watery names that confirm
The dryness of their ways.
To visit the places of occlusion, or the lick
In a vlei-bank dawn.
To bury my mouth in the pit of your arm,
In that planetarium,
Pectoral beginning to the nub of time
Down there close to the water-table, to feel
The full moon as it drums
At the back of my throat
Its cow-skinned vowel.
To write a poem with words like:
I'm telling you,
Stompie, stickfast, golovan,
Songololo, just boombang, just
To understand the least inflections,
To voice without swallowing
Syllables born in tin shacks, or catch
the 5.15 ikwata bust fife
Chwannisberg train, to reach

The low chant of the mine gang's
Mineral glow of our people's unbreakable resolve.

To learn how to speak
With the voices of this land.

JEREMY CRONIN

from Walking on Air

from the Prologue

In the prison workshop, also known as the seminar room;

In the seminar room, sawdust up the nose, feet in plane shavings, old jam tins on racks, a dropped plank, planks, a stack of mason's floats waiting assembly, Warder von Loggerenberg sitting in the corner;

In the prison workshop, also and otherwise named, where work is done by enforced dosage, between political discussion, theoretical discussion, tactical discussion, bemoaning of life without women, sawdust up the nose, while raging at bench 4, for a week long, a discussion raging, above the hum of the exhaust fans, on how to distinguish the concept "Productive" from the concept . . . "Unproductive Labour";

In the prison workshop then, over the months, over the screech of the grindstone, I'm asking John Matthews about his life and times, as I crank the handle, he's sharpening a plane blade, holding it up in the light to check on its bevel, dipping the blade to cool in a tin of water, then back to the grindstone, sparks fly: "I work for myself" — he says — "not for the boere";

In the prison workshop, with John Matthews making contraband goeters, boxes, ashtrays, smokkel salt cellars of, oh, delicate dovetailings;

Over the months, then, in the prison workshop, I'm asking John Matthews, while he works intently, he likes manual work, he likes the feel of woodgrain, he doesn't like talking too much, the making and fixing of things he likes, he likes, agh no, hayikona, slap-bang-bang, work for the jailers;

In the prison workshop, then, I ask John Matthews, was he present on the two days of Kliptown . . . 1955? . . . when the People's Congress adopted the Freedom Charter?

Actually

No he wasn't

He was there the day before, he built the platform

In the prison workshop, then, over the hum of exhaust fans, between the knocking in of nails, the concept "Productive," the concept "Unproductive Labour," feet in plane shavings, John Matthews speaks by snatches, the making and fixing of things he likes, though much, never, much you won't catch him speaking;

But here, pieced together, here from many months, from the prison workshop

Here is one comrade's story.

~

Born to Bez Valley, Joburg
into the last of his jail term
stooped now he has grown

In this undernourished frame
that dates back
to those first years of his life.

He was nine
when his father came
blacklisted home

From the 1922
Rand Revolt,
and there was a makeshift

Forge in their backyard
a never again to be employed
father passed on to his son

A lifelong
love for the making
and fixing of things.

From Bez Valley it was,
veiled like a bride in fine
mine-dump dust

He went out
to whom it may concern
comma

A dependable lad
comma
his spelling is good.

At fifteen he became
office boy at Katzenellenbogen's
cnr. von Wielligh

And President streets
where he earned: £1 a week,
where he learned:

* Good spelling doesn't always count.
* The GPO telegram charge is reckoned per word.
* A word is 15 letters max.
* You have to drop ONE *l* from Katzenellenbogen Inc or
        HEAR ME BOY?! nex' time
        YOU'S gonna pay extra one word
            charge your bliksem self.

And the recession came
but he got a bookkeeping job
with Kobe Silk

On the same block
        — John Edward
Matthews . . .

ANDRIES WALTER OLIPHANT

Childhood in Heidelberg

I was born in a house where ancestors
were suspended from the walls.
On hot afternoons
they would descend and walk silently
through the cool passages
of the dark house, slowly
as if strolling through a womb.

The roof is a vantage point for birds and pigeons.
On the stoep
in an ancient folding chair my namesake sits.
There is a giant gumtree
at the gate in which the sun sets.
The stars are candles
which my grandmother has lit.

Every morning father wakes to find a man
with a hole in his head
sleeping in the driftsand
of the furrow which runs
along the creosoted split-pole fence.
I go in search of the orchestra of crickets.

In the kitchen mother cries as she turns
the toast on the black plates
of the Welcome Dover.
When father packed my pigeons into boxes,
I ended up with Rover and the cats
on the back of a truck

with all the household goods.
I thought, if this is part of life, it's fun.

At the end of the truck's journey
through the sky, we arrived
in a toy town of match-box houses,
lined up like tombstones in a graveyard.
At once, I understood why my mother cried.

KELWYN SOLE
Conjunction

I imagine you naked.

Your hand reaches out
and touches me again
so fleetingly
for the third time —

I can think of no thing
to say, but smile, and offer you
another piece of bread
dipped in hummus,
dripping

and the way out of this party.

How shall I ask?

Through denim
our hips touch, rub

then you do:

heart
jags in my throat

∼

The words, the words
that have all evening risen

in their balloons
                    pop

giggling little explosions of sound as
I follow you upwards

past your mother
and my imagined mother

my face flicks through dark striations
curds of light
from the bulb outside your door
eat your face

the stairs creak and utter
with the weight of what
we cannot see

~

On the small pine table
hugged close to your bed
our clothes gradually embrace
one by one
                    I feel
myself flicker as night stills
on my puckering skin

you light a single candle

in the darkness

the tiny flame reels:

shadows nudging and
flowing across the walls

~

        My fingers
nibble you like questing mice. Bump
against your shirt's buttons

fumble behind your back and tug
so your breasts bounce
as you shrug
free, goosepimpling

on my buckle
the cuticle of your nail tears

night fattens
roots and grunts through
the tropic of our bellies

~

Your breasts swell to the dunes
up which my footsteps plod.
                A skittering
of sand behind the heel. I take
      your heel in my hand
      and push upward,

level to the other knee
                    the clock ticks
                    you sigh
as I lick higher, past inner thigh,
through the coarse fur where
your smell beckons. Each
            stroke of the tongue finds wet hair
and flesh, pink flap at the centre
            nut-whorled. Hips shift:
the clock moans:

your legs on my shoulders
apant in the desert of dreams

~

The archipelago of your tongue
licks me. I am ocean now,

entirely salt,
boneless
            as moist with lust we
seep towards bedrock, slip
into twining depths

where we cannot see, then can see

~

I reach
upwards

loosened you bob
to the surface to sponge up
air

make me gasp for air

our bodies push, luxuriate
thighs fight to gain a stranglehold
and move faster now, en-
circling

breath rippling across silence

~

l rise to you:
you shift your rump
                    up
languorously
            breasts hanging
            my mouth open
our movements swim in thick oil
only the dry sound of your heart
stops and pulses l
                slip in
slowly to your mucus and the heat, slowly
                gripped
                        my vision tips
forming a new white architecture

we slide through the night, riding

~

In your tucked legs'
junction
the hair glistens
lustrous, bespattered:

breath slows, catches
in our throats
and sours. Tumbles
on your hands gone
inert as scattered leaves

     settles
on softening nipples, my cock
lounging sticky on your thigh

through the smudge of black
lush in your armpit
dawn shifts

~

Do we uphold these moments
               against death?
        The clock purrs
in the corner and washes its face,
pretends not to notice

our separate limbs begin to stir
but we grin at each other
as we dress
for within this new, backfiring,
quarrelsome day

our composure holds a secret:

love comes back to us
and whispers
through the tides of our blood
with the orbits of our bodies

again and again and again

INGRID DE KOK
Our Sharpeville

I was playing hopscotch on the slate
when miners roared past in lorries,
their arms raised, signals at a crossing,
their chanting foreign and familiar,
like the call and answer of road gangs
across the veld, building hot arteries
from the heart of the Transvaal mine.

I ran to the gate to watch them pass.
And it seemed like a great caravan
moving across the desert to an oasis
I remembered from my Sunday School book:
olive trees, a deep jade pool,
men resting in clusters after a long journey,
the danger of the mission still around them,
and night falling, its silver stars just like the ones
you got for remembering your Bible texts.

Then my grandmother called from behind the front door,
her voice a stiff broom over the steps:
"Come inside; they do things to little girls."

For it was noon, and there was no jade pool.
Instead, a pool of blood that already had a living name
and grew like a shadow as the day lengthened.
The dead, buried in voices that reached even my gate,
the chanting men on the ambushed trucks,
these were not heroes in my town,
but maulers of children,

doing things that had to remain nameless.
And our Sharpeville was this fearful thing
that might tempt us across the wellswept streets.

If I had turned I would have seen
brocade curtains drawn tightly across sheer net ones,
known there were eyes behind both,
heard the dogs pacing in the locked yard next door.
But, walking backwards, all I felt was shame,
at being a girl, at having been found at the gate,
at having heard my grandmother lie
and at my fear her lie might be true.
Walking backwards, called back,
I returned to the closed rooms, home.

INGRID DE KOK

Small Passing

(For a woman whose baby died stillborn, and who was told by a
man to stop mourning, "because the trials and horrors suffered
daily by black women in this country are more significant than the
loss of one white child.")

I

In this country you may not
suffer the death of your stillborn,
remember the last push into shadow and silence,
the useless wires and cords on your stomach,
the nurse's face, the walls, the afterbirth in a basin.
Do not touch your breasts
still full of purpose.
Do not circle the house,
pack, unpack the small clothes.
Do not lie awake at night hearing
the doctor say "It was just as well"
and "You can have another."
In this country you may not
mourn small passings.

See: the newspaper boy in the rain
will sleep tonight in a doorway.
The woman in the busline
may next month be on a train
to a place not her own.
The baby in the backyard now
will be sent to a tired aunt,

grow chubby, then lean,
return a stranger.
Mandela's daughter tried to find her father
through the glass. She thought they'd let her touch him.

And this woman's hands are so heavy when she dusts
the photographs of other children
they fall to the floor and break.
Clumsy woman, she moves so slowly
as if in a funeral rite.

On the pavements the nannies meet.
These are legal gatherings.
They talk about everything, about home,
while the children play among them,
their skins like litmus, their bonnets clean.

2

Small wrist in the grave.
Baby no one carried live
between houses, among trees.
Child shot running,
stones in his pocket,
boy's swollen stomach
full of hungry air.
Girls carrying babies
not much smaller than themselves.
Erosion. Soil washed down to the sea.

3

I think these mothers dream
headstones of the unborn.
Their mourning rises like a wall
no vine will cling to.
They will not tell you your suffering is white.
They will not say it is just as well.
They will not compete for the ashes of infants.
I think they may say to you:
Come with us to the place of mothers.
We will stroke your flat empty belly,
let you weep with us in the dark,
and arm you with one of our babies
to carry home on your back.

KELWYN SOLE
Blessing

I

I was at home
that day because
of unrest at
the school. My mother

said to help her.
At noon she left
our house: she
took a bus to town.

I was in her room,
closely listening to the radio
When I saw
the thing happen.

A bakkie in the street
— it was white and yellow —
stopped before
my eyes.

I noticed it and
the sight was very
fearful for me.
My friends at school

ran when they saw
that one and named
it as "the cobra."
I saw the driver

struggling with
another man who
hit out as he fled
from the passenger

side. He ran
nearby our house
with the driver
following, very fast.

The driver was
carrying a small gun
like a pistol;
two other persons also

jumped out the back
of the truck
and ran as well. They
were all chasing

the man without a weapon.
These other two were
also armed. The man
held a shotgun

and the woman
a butcher's knife
she waved around
above her head.

I will never forget
the woman especially
I saw she had
a pale complexion

and had her hair
caught up in a beautiful
green doek. She wore
her jeans extremely

tight so she ran
slower than the others,
after them,
following the man.

2

I saw the chase
was going to end
badly. The person

running away
was somewhat fat
and a little bit old

possibly, because
his hair on top
was getting thin.

He ran into our
small backyard and I
lost sight of him.

Our friend Ludidi
who was watching
also by this time

shouted from next door
"jump over, jump over"
but the fence

was very much too high
for that man. He
ran around the house

onto our stoep,
nearly in front
of the opened window

that I stood behind.
By now I could
not cry out and

couldn't even move.
I could hear him
panting noisily his

weeping as he
tripped. The man
with the pistol

caught up with him
at last and shouted
out in triumph

as he bent down
over him. The
shotgun person

appeared also
and both of them
shot him

in the back — many
times — very close.
I heard eight

or nine in all.
Each time the body
of the fallen man

would jump a little
from the concrete
on which he now

was lying. The woman
joined the men
and put her knife

close to his throat,
saying, "let
me cut him,

let me cut him!"
The men shook their
heads but laughed.

3

They turned to leave.
Our neighbour,
who is a foolish

somebody shouted
"who have you killed,
who are you
going to leave

here like a dog
in a ditch?" The man
I thought was dead

slowly stirred his
neck, whispered
"I am of
Xokozela." As

he spoke bubbles
of blood came from
his mouth then

his mouth
opened very wide.
Then his head
fell down again.

But they took his arms
his feet and
threw him in the

vehicle. This
is all I saw,
I can say nothing
more except

my brother told me later
he had seen the
three were eating

fish and chips that
afternoon next to
Mabunu's, and
joking in loud voices.

Their bakkie wasn't
with them there it
stood further down the road

doors wide open in front
of the police station.
Zanele said he could
still see the stains

on one man's shirt. At
the time he thought it
must be food that spilt.

4

My mother says
her soul has always
fed itself from off
my name but now

I'm changed before
her very eyes. I laugh
and tease no more

and do not seem
to want to look
and do not
seem to want

to look at all
out of the window.

TATAMKHULU AFRIKA

Dark Rider

I go up into the kloof sometimes:
it is quiet there with the trees gathering like clouds,
and only the moon moves.

I lie there on the green turf and the air sings:
crickets or winds or a far bird,
and I feel like a man on an island
who hears the sea all around him,
and is comforted by the circle of it,
and yet is afraid to put out his hand,
finding there not the rushing of seawater,
but the desolate breath of the void.

The city is not far from there:
I come from it in a few minutes on the hot nights,
but there are no roads to bear its dissonance
and the shoulder of the mountain shrugs away its lights.

Flowers are but few,
but there is a great greenness and a rich earth
and when the dew lies heavily upon it,
it smells far sweeter than any flower could.

All is not softness though:
there are thickets of dead wood like thick smoke,
rising, silently, between the green,
or grey hairs being shed by the still living trees,
and at the mouth of the glade there is a dead pine,
and sometimes an owl booms.

And sometimes also, when I lie still,
I hear the dark rider passing by,
the whisper of his cloak in the wet grass, the scuff of a hoof on a stone,
and all night then, waking now and again,
I will be aware of him moving in the glade,
a flash of starlight on a buckle, the white moth of a hand,
and towards dawn,
I will see him sitting at the foot of the dead pine,
silent as a sentinel, his face forever not seen.

And although I know well there is no one there,
I have a right to my dream,
a dream like a child's
of the night and a watcher whose face turns aside . . .

JEREMY CRONIN

from Running Towards Us

. . . The victory of life over death? Of the innocent small person caught in the middle?

But what is the middle?

Are you sure, in the thick of all this slaughter, he could be innocent?

Whom did he just betray? Whom will he still betray now as he runs away from the executioners?

Away from the spectators. Away from the police and army with fresh killings on their hands. A corpse covered in petrol, each stumbling pace one step more away from a death it has already died.

He is running towards us. Into our exile. Into the return of exiles. Running towards the negotiated settlement. Towards the democratic elections. He is running, sore, into the new South Africa. Into our rainbow nation, in desperation, one shoe on, one shoe off. Into our midst. Running.

KELWYN SOLE
Housing Targets

Somewhere in our past
we believed in the future

that a better world
would discover foundation
under our feet, and we
would be forever singing,
in its kitchen.

Bricks pile up in a field.
Whether they will be enough
no one knows. How
they fit together
is anyone's guess.

Men with darkening skins
scribbled on by weather
wait for their instructions.

From time to time
limousines miraculously appear:
there is always a somebody
in a suit willing to smile
and shake their hands

who lays the first stone.

Then the camera lights
and racing engines

turn around, shrink back
from where they came.

Those left behind
stare at their own hands
afterwards, puzzled
at precisely what
has been transacted, why
they are still being offered
bonds

      squint
between gnarled fingers
pace out the hopeful distances:
— there will be a flower bowl.
— my bed is going here.

As for now the doorknobs
have no doors.

Their windows peer out
at no sky.

THE ANTIPODES: AUSTRALIA

CURATED BY LES MURRAY

CAIRNS BIRDWING
ORNITHOPTERA EUPHORION

MARY GILMORE
Bones in a Pot

Little Billy Button
Said he wanted mutton;
Miss Betty Bligh
Said she wanted pie;
But young Johnny Jones
Said he wanted Bones —
Bones in a pot,
    All hot!

LESBIA HARFORD

[I'm like all lovers]

I'm like all lovers, wanting love to be
A very mighty thing for you and me.

In certain moods your love should be a fire
That burnt your very life up in desire.

The only kind of love, then, to my mind
Would make you kiss my shadow on the blind

And walk seven miles each night to see it there.
Myself within, serene and unaware.

But you're as bad. You'd have me watch the clock
And count your coming while I mend your sock.

You'd have my mind devoted day and night
To you and care for you and your delight.

Poor fools, who each would have the other give
What spirit must withhold if it would live.

You're not my slave, I wish you not to be.
I love yourself and not your love for me,

The self that goes ten thousand miles away
And loses thought of me for many a day.

And you loved me for loving much beside
But now you want a woman for your bride.

Oh, make no woman of me, you who can,
Or I will make a husband of a man.

By my unwomanly love that sets you free
Love all myself, but least the woman in me.

JUDITH WRIGHT

Legend

The blacksmith's boy went out with a rifle
and a black dog running behind.
Cobwebs snatched at his feet,
rivers hindered him,
thorn-branches caught at his eyes to make him blind
and the sky turned into an unlucky opal,
but he didn't mind.
I can break branches, I can swim rivers, I can stare out any spider
      I meet,
said he to his dog and his rifle.

The blacksmith's boy went over the paddocks
with his old black hat on his head.
Mountains jumped in his way,
rocks rolled down on him,
and the old crow cried, You'll soon be dead;
and the rain came down like mattocks.
But he only said
I can climb mountains, I can dodge rocks, I can shoot an old crow
      any day.
And he went on over the paddocks.

When he came to the end of the day the sun began falling.
Up came the night ready to swallow him,
like the barrel of a gun,
like an old black hat,
like a black dog hungry to follow him.

Then the pigeon, the magpie and the dove began wailing,
and the grass lay down to pillow him.
His rifle broke, his hat blew away and his dog was gone,
and the sun was falling.

But in front of the night the rainbow stood on the mountain
just as his heart foretold.
He ran like a hare,
he climbed like a fox,
he caught it in his hands, the colours and the cold —
like a bar of ice, like the column of a fountain,
like a ring of gold.
The pigeon, the magpie and the dove flew up to stare,
and the grass stood up again on the mountain.

The blacksmith's boy hung the rainbow on his shoulder,
instead of his broken gun.
Lizards ran out to see,
snakes made way for him,
and the rainbow shone as brightly as the sun.
All the world said, Nobody is braver, nobody is bolder,
nobody else has done
anything to equal it. He went home as easy as could be
with the swinging rainbow on his shoulder.

BILLY MARSHALL STONEKING
The Seasons of Fire

There is Law for Fire,
singing for Fire,
dancing for Fire —
Fire Dreaming.
You have been there, you have seen it.
You know all the names of Fire;
signal fires, hunting fires,
sleeping fires, fires for light,
fires for cooking, for ceremonies,
healing fires of eucalyptus leaves —
Fire is medicine,   magic.
        Fire gave Crow a voice,
flying away in pain.
Fire brings old quarrels to an end.
On top of Uluru,   do not drink
At the rockhole of Warnampi
unless you take Fire
or the snake will bite your spirit
and drought will follow.
Fire can protect you from the dead ones.

You have been there, you have seen them.
You know all this Fire.
The penis is Fire.
The vagina is Fire.
Fire is inside the bodies of animals.
The woman hands a firestick to the boy
and he becomes a man.
There is a time for every fire.
The fires of January are different

from the fires of June.
In the cold time, a small nudge before sleep
will keep the flame alive all night.
The right ash, the right heat,
the right position of wind, dune and saltbush:
a technology of Fire. The knowledge.

You have been there, you have watched.
You know all the seasons of Fire.
     Hawk stopped Bush Turkey
throwing Fire into the sea.
Fire cannot be stolen now;   it lives
Everywhere — inside the spinifex and dry wood.
All this is Law.
"The smoking days" — Buyuguyunya — come every year.
The air is full of smoke.
The smoke comes first, then the fire,
and then the smoke.
All this is Law.
Hot is more than two sticks rubbed together; and
no chopping — take only what you can drag:
green wood for shelter;
dead pieces for waru.
The wind from the mouth works kindling.
Fire makes grass seed.
It finds the kangaroo   and chases him
to the hunters.
All this is Law.
The burning off and the gathering together are one.

You have been there, you have seen it.
You know all the seasons of Fire.

ROBERT GRAY

Among the Mountains of Guang-xi Province in Southern China

I had been wading for a long while in the sands of the world
and was buffeted by its fiery winds,
then I found myself carried on a bamboo raft (I am speaking
    literally now),
poled by a boatman down the Li River.

A guest in Beijing at the Central Academy of Arts,
brought to the countryside,
I'd wandered out alone. A sheen on the night and across the ranks
    of water,
and close mountains that joined smoky earth and sky.

When I saw the landscape around Guilin city
and realised it was the same as the painter Shi Tao had known it
I felt suddenly exalted,
as though I were riding in the saddle of a cloud.

The mountains' outlines were crowded one behind another
and seemed a wild loosening of the brush,
a switchback scrubbing, rounded or angular,
until the last fibres of the ink had been used up, again and again.

Those narrow blue mountains make endless configurations.
They are by far the main crop the province bears.
Chuang Tzu said that a twisted tree is not useful
and so it can survive for a thousand years.

A lead star plunged behind the mountains
as if the galaxy were crumbling more quickly than them.
How to convey the strangeness of this region?
I thought of migrating whales that break together, almost upright,
out of the sea.

That suggests their power, but not their stillness.
Some mountains reminded me of tall-hatted mushrooms,
some of veiled women, among a laden caravan, but all had a
corroded edging of trees.
We drifted by a few other rafts and their lanterns.

At times I saw rhinoceros horns, or a blackened cathedral;
at times the beauty of an old carnivorous jawbone.
One place was as dramatic as a vertical wind-sock.
There was a broken palace in a fog-bound wilderness.

The next day we travelled to the village of Xin Ping
and found there drabness and squalor, a terrible indifference and
listlessness.
Worst of all, the poverty in people's faces,
the smallness of those lives. Everything was the colour of dust and
of smoke.

How can they not be embittered, and millions with them?
They see the comfort of cities, each night, on the communal
television,
just hours off, and behind a stone door.
Earth could not bear the waste, were they to have a fraction of
what they know.

We who'd alighted there, for a few days,
could love nature because of its indifference, and found our
    freedom in that.
To do so, one must be secure. The same type of mountains were at
    Xin Ping
but I saw in them the sadness of eternal things.

JOHN FORBES
Malta

The sky was carpeted with Italian flak. Crump!
It explodes in the war comic. "Stone the crows"
We think "That was close." Closer than we think
They sing "If ever a wiz there was it's that
Wonderful wizard of Oz" or "Circuits & bumps & loops
Laddie & how to get out of a spin." Maria Schneider
Says: "Tu es cet homme." I loop the loop. "Wizard
Prang, Red Leader!" exclaims the Wing Commander
"Want a beer?" All this helps the war along. We
Fight the Hearts & Minds campaign. For instance,
"My heart throbs inside a sandbagged blast-pen
But a lousy dumbness holds my tongue. It's a matter
Of mind over matter, my head avoiding the matter
Cradled in the space between your tits." I'm not
But the aircrew are trained for this. They kept
Australia free. That is, up to scratch — not
Spectacular, but par for the course ("The sky was
Carpeted . . ." etc.) I hope you can see this. It's
A picture of my father who almost flew a bomber.
Up close he looks like me — both cocky, a cigarette
Balanced on the edge of the intense inane. This comic
Is called "Torpedoes Running." Then later, over
Malta in a terminal spin, I throw away the rule book
& bring her in. Then a terrific Italian raid begins.

PETER GOLDSWORTHY

Alcohol

You are the eighth
and shallowest
of the seven seas,

a shriveled fragmented ocean
dispersed into bottles, kegs, casks,
warm puddles in lanes behind pubs:
a chain of ponds.

Also a kind of spa,
a very hot spring:
medicinal water to be taken
before meals, with meals, after meals,
without meals;

chief cure
for gout, dropsy, phlegm,
bad humours, apoplexy, rheumatism
and chief cause of all the same.

At best you make a lovely mischief:
wetter of cunts,
drooper of cocks.

At worst you never know when to stop:
wife-beater, mugger of innocents,
chief mitigating circumstance
for half the evil in the world.

All of which I know too well
but choose to ignore,
remembering each night only this advice:
never eat on an empty stomach;

for always you make me a child again —
sentimental, boring
and for one happy hour very happy —
sniffing out my true character like a dog:
my Sea of Tranquility,
always exactly shallow enough to drown in.

JENNIFER COMPTON

From the other woman left under the pillow

. . . he is a lovely man has a lovely thing smiles with his eyes & mouth
you saw him first but I would have if I'd been there
he is a lovely man sweet as honey his thing is plums & rose petals
I know all there is, you know, about him, know about you
I walk into your house I have walked into your home
"You crazy bitch get your gear off *si tu veux*"
pardonnez-moi we speak French which you speak better than me
but here I am I've found a place in his heart your home
I'm drinking coffee he is naked & you are just around the corner
I could snatch my hand back not without opening it & letting go
displacement has taken place eureka we all found each other
he likes you so he couldn't like me as much without liking you conundrum
it's always two out of three with the other round the corner
in a corner of his heart his heart the shuttlecock
not us not me & you my sister *ma semblable ma soeur*
we are not together him the net we speak through touch fingers perhaps
we desire each other he carries our love for each other back & forward
our passionate messenger we fill him up so he spills us into each other . . .

PHILIP HODGINS
Midday Horizon

The summer's worn-out paddocks
aligned as neatly as quatrains on a page,
one of those highly buffed duco skies,
and in between, a fine graph line
as nervy as a lot of black snakes in the heat.
Great sheets of mirage are lying there
as bright as new galvo.
You squint into the glare until your eyes
are nothing more than two short twitching lines
and see on the horizon
the standing shadow of a eucalyptus tree.
A big mob of sheep is moving to the left,
breaking up and catching up
in slow eddies like a lava flow.
Seen through the hot distorting air
clear flames seem to be tearing off the mob.
A man is walking sheep-slow behind them.
From where you are
his shape is continually being modified
as if he were walking through different dimensions.
Sometimes he seems to slip into separate pieces,
then pull back together, temporarily.
The same thing is happening to the tree.
The man stops
and a low piece of him draws right away this time.
It must be a dog.
You notice the silence, how near it is.
There's no threat that you can see
and yet the thin exposed horizon trembles.

ASHLLEY MORGAN - SHAE

Edinburgh

Up, down, tower round
So many steps in Edinburgh
Streets all end in a friendly bar
Tour-guides spruik, all costume-gowned
"We have a real ghost," for ten pound
"Bide a while here," rim ram rah

August fireworks shoot up stars
It's push and shove to get out far
The Royal Mile of hungry Fringe hounds
Up, down, tower round

Museum on each cobbled tar
Fairy-floss, side-stalls and tea-jar
On Princes' green, fat seagulls mound
Castle, cathedral, uphill wound
History theme park, dum-dee-dah
Up, down, tower round

Turrets on top, streets underground
Keystone cabs, tipsy buses sound
Old books, wee cups, candelabra
Royal Yacht Britannia, oomp-pah-pah
Unicorn rules — ground-chained and crowned
Up, down, tower round

A gene-link, tartan, gravestone found
Plague-street, proclaimed witch torture-bound

The Covenanter's last hurrah
So many steps in Edinburgh
Up, down, tower round

KENNETH SLESSOR

Five Bells

Time that is moved by little fidget wheels
Is not my Time, the flood that does not flow.
Between the double and the single bell
Of a ship's hour, between a round of bells
From the dark warship riding there below,
I have lived many lives, and this one life
Of Joe, long dead, who lives between five bells.

Deep and dissolving verticals of light
Ferry the falls of moonshine down. Five bells
Coldly rung out in a machine's voice. Night and water
Pour to one rip of darkness, the Harbour floats
In air, the Cross hangs upside-down in water.

Why do I think of you, dead man, why thieve
These profitless lodgings from the flukes of thought
Anchored in Time? You have gone from earth,
Gone even from the meaning of a name;
Yet something's there, yet something forms its lips
And hits and cries against the ports of space,
Beating their sides to make its fury heard.

Are you shouting at me, dead man, squeezing your face
In agonies of speech on speechless panes?
Cry louder, beat the windows, bawl your name!

But I hear nothing, nothing . . . only bells,
Five bells, the bumpkin calculus of Time.
Your echoes die, your voice is dowsed by Life,

There's not a mouth can fly the pygmy strait —
Nothing except the memory of some bones
Long shoved away, and sucked away, in mud;
And unimportant things you might have done,
Or once I thought you did; but you forgot,
And all have now forgotten — looks and words
And slops of beer; your coat with buttons off,
Your gaunt chin and pricked eye, and raging tales
Of Irish kings and English perfidy,
And dirtier perfidy of publicans
Groaning to God from Darlinghurst.

Five bells.

Then I saw the road, I heard the thunder
Tumble, and felt the talons of the rain
The night we came to Moorebank in slab-dark,
So dark you bore no body, had no face,
But a sheer voice that rattled out of air
(As now you'd cry if I could break the glass),
A voice that spoke beside me in the bush,
Loud for a breath or bitten off by wind,
Of Milton, melons, and the Rights of Man,
And blowing flutes, and how Tahitian girls
Are brown and angry-tongued, and Sydney girls
Are white and angry-tongued, or so you'd found.
But all I heard was words that didn't join
So Milton became melons, melons girls,
And fifty mouths, it seemed, were out that night,
And in each tree an Ear was bending down,
Or something had just run, gone behind grass,

When, blank and bone-white, like a maniac's thought,
The naphtha-flash of lightning slit the sky,
Knifing the dark with deathly photographs.
There's not so many with so poor a purse
Or fierce a need, must fare by night like that,
Five miles in darkness on a country track,
But when you do, that's what you think.

                    Five bells.

In Melbourne, your appetite had gone,
Your angers too; they had been leeched away
By the soft archery of summer rains
And the sponge-paws of wetness, the slow damp
That stuck the leaves of living, snailed the mind,
And showed your bones, that had been sharp with rage,
The sodden ecstasies of rectitude.
I thought of what you'd written in faint ink,
Your journal with the sawn-off lock, that stayed behind
With other things you left, all without use,
All without meaning now, except a sign
That someone had been living who now was dead:
"At Labassa. Room 6 x 8
On top of the tower; because of this, very dark
And cold in winter. Everything has been stowed
Into this room — 500 books all shapes
And colours, dealt across the floor
And over sills and on the laps of chairs;
Guns, photoes of many differant things
And differant curioes that I obtained . . ."

In Sydney, by the spent aquarium-flare
Of penny gaslight on pink wallpaper,
We argued about blowing up the world,
But you were living backward, so each night
You crept a moment closer to the breast,
And they were living, all of them, those frames
And shapes of flesh that had perplexed your youth,
And most your father, the old man gone blind,
With fingers always round a fiddle's neck,
That graveyard mason whose fair monuments
And tablets cut with dreams of piety
Rest on the bosoms of a thousand men
Staked bone by bone, in quiet astonishment
At cargoes they had never thought to bear,
These funeral-cakes of sweet and sculptured stone.

Where have you gone? The tide is over you,
The turn of midnight water's over you,
As Time is over you, and mystery,
And memory, the flood that does not flow.
You have no suburb, like those easier dead
In private berths of dissolution laid —
The tide goes over, the waves ride over you
And let their shadows down like shining hair,
But they are Water; and the sea-pinks bend
Like lilies in your teeth, but they are Weed;
And you are only part of an Idea.
I felt the wet push its black thumb-balls in,
The night you died, I felt your eardrums crack,
And the short agony, the longer dream,
The Nothing that was neither long nor short;

But I was bound, and could not go that way,
But I was blind, and could not feel your hand.
If I could find an answer, could only find
Your meaning, or could say why you were here
Who now are gone, what purpose gave you breath
Or seized it back, might I not hear your voice?

I looked out my window in the dark
At waves with diamond quills and combs of light
That arched their mackerel-backs and smacked the sand
In the moon's drench, that straight enormous glaze,
And ships far off asleep, and Harbour-buoys
Tossing their fireballs wearily each to each,
And tried to hear your voice, but all I heard
Was a boat's whistle, and the scraping squeal
Of seabirds' voices far away, and bells,
Five bells. Five bells coldly ringing out.

Five bells.

ALAN GOULD

from The End of Sail, 1924–1939

Galaxies

Hamburg; the clockhands move upon their star.
A liner glides along the Elbe, its lights
move through the city's lights, a galaxy
passing in silence through a galaxy.

My girl's behind me on the bed. She smokes
and minutes tick. Her time is waiting for
a time to end, a time to start. As mine is.
We are the flowers of our lineage,

were sinuous, bluff-mannered in the wine-room
with all our company at like pursuits,
transactions that the liquor tantalized,
that led into this silence and this calm.

Yes, here I took myself, yes, here was taken.
And here she chose to lie and here was laid.
Our choices and our fates, we house them both
like galaxies that pass through one another.

The liner disappears behind the docklands;
my girl is getting dressed again behind me.
I'll close the curtain on this night sky's map,
step out into the dark I know knows me.

MARGARET HARVEY
Living in M—ls&B—n

I wish I lived in M—ls&B—n
I would be lithe with long legs
and could have red hair and a name like Flame
without anybody laughing.
Whenever I'd get together with Hugh/Roderick/Harrington,
trails of tiny kisses would go just about everywhere
and he would be able
to do extraordinary things to my bust.
Nobody in M—ls&B—n takes it amiss
when things suddenly harden or go soft.
Things open a great deal too,
and buttons go flying all over the place —
in fact the undoing of fastenings and tearing of silks
are the main occupations of the inhabitants
if you don't count the sudden taking-in of breaths.
If I lived in M—ls&B—n
I would have a touch of fire and make his eyes glitter —
mine, of course, would widen, as a heroine's eyes do
when other things harden or open.
M—ls&B—n is a lovely place,
either Majorca or a big hospital or the Outback,
or a small hospital in the Outback.
I can be anyone, but he must have a mouth that can harden
or open, or soften, and is usually claiming mine.
In M—ls&B—n a lot of claiming goes on —
it's the men who are so possessive.
As well, they are thirty-six, tall, dark,
and their eyes have been known to turn into silver slits
under the strain of all that hardening.

If I lived in M—ls&B—n
I would stay delectable forever,
but, with a strongly curved mouth always claiming mine,
and a hand constantly at my fastenings,
perhaps I don't want to live in M—ls&B—n.

JEAN FRANCES
Short Fall

when I hear of those
who don't make it

the failed priest
who can never return
to the family fold in Ireland

the London student
on her way back to Illinois
leaping from the ship's rail
rather than lose face
in her home town

the schoolgirl in Japan
who slashes her wrists
when she comes second in her class

I think of my friend
aspiring to excellence
only to miss his goal
who with a rueful grin
took a gun
from the glove box of his car
and tossed it into the river
as he crossed the bridge

TOM COVERDALE
Woodwind

My didjeridoo Nibelungenlied
wallows brooding as Wagner's did.
You point to where your back is sore;
I press the didj to the spot and pour
into the knotted muscle moans,
half words, half-animal groans.

Through the wood your responses come.
Who? An Austrian long from home.
What? A sprite playing hide and seek.
When? A week, I'll be gone next week.
Where? My home — you knew I would.
I miss the wood, my wood.

THE ANTIPODES: AOTEAROA/ NEW ZEALAND

CURATED BY HINEMOANA BAKER

NEW ZEALAND RED ADMIRAL
KAHUKURA/VANESSA GONEPILLA

HONE TUWHARE

No Ordinary Sun

Tree let your arms fall:
raise them not sharply in supplication
to the bright enhaloed cloud.
Let your arms lack toughness and
resilience for this is no mere axe
to blunt, nor fire to smother.

Your sap shall not rise again
to the moon's pull.
No more incline a deferential head
to the wind's talk, or stir
to the tickle of coursing rain.

Your former shagginess shall not be
wreathed with the delightful flight
of birds nor shield
nor cool the ardour of unheeding
lovers from the monstrous sun.

Tree let your naked arms fall
nor extend vain entreaties to the radiant ball.
This is no gallant monsoon's flash,
no dashing trade wind's blast.
The fading green of your magic
emanations shall not make pure again
these polluted skies . . . for this
is no ordinary sun.

O tree
in the shadowless mountains

the white plains and
the drab sea floor
your end at last is written.

ROBERT SULLIVAN

Waka 99

If waka could be resurrected
they wouldn't just come out
from museum doors smashing
glass cases revolving and sliding
doors on their exit

they wouldn't just come out
of mountains as if liquefied
from a frozen state
the resurrection wouldn't just
come about this way

the South Island turned to wood
waiting for the giant crew
of Maui and his brothers
bailers and anchors turned back
to what they were when they were strewn

about the country by Kupe
and his relations
the resurrection would happen
in the blood of the men and women
the boys and girls

who are blood relations
of the crews whose veins
touch the veins who touched the veins
of those who touched the veins
who touched the veins

who touched the veins
of the men and women from the time
of Kupe and before.
The resurrection will come
out of their blood.

MARTY SMITH

The Stolen

(Urewera Mural, Park Headquarters, Lake Waikaremoana)

> *At the boundary can I forbear to turn my head?*
> —Colin McCahon

I

I lost the huia feather, passed down to my mother,
in the bush behind our house.
The feather fell out of my hair, and out
of the known world.
Sent back, I was a kereru
stumbling, bashing through bushes
but every feather was black and white,
it was all meaning without colour,
only the feathers of magpie.

2

Like the dam you build in the creek with sticks,
two thousand years ago, a huge mass
of mud and rocks slid off the cliffs
of Ngāmoko and blocked the river gorge at Panekiri.
The weight of water, the drowned —
on a clean day the petrified trees
stretch their shapes, shimmer
deep down to dark.

   2,000 feet above sea level

the lake rocks hold, tower over
the metal road that winds up from Wairoa.
Laid down in ash, flames could still
could still, flames could roar out the cracks
in the earth vents. Waikaremoana could rush
Wairoa into the sea.

3

Flag riding red above the bluffs,
Te Kooti swam the horses, people, all,
through the narrows and vanished.
The broadleaf and ferns silent,
still dark bush thoughts,
rain red-fingered along the sky light.

4

So dark and cold, said the woman, why did they
put the Visitors' Centre up there in the bush?
And that painting, she said, it's so gloomy
at least he got the colours right.

The stolen McCahon again
haloed in yellow-white when the sun strikes through
spears of indrawn breath
light drifts and shifts
with mist and rain
Tuhoe, the dark forest and the tree

driven by light riding upwards
the tired sun breaking
red light riding fast across the bluff tops, the one
narrowing in, is this the one they said would come —
Rua Kenana
weaving flax like networks
the green of the deep still lake
still water after the sun has gone

I turned off the light.
The great white trunk rising, bark battered,
the flags protested, their crazy colour said no
and all the while the light burned out of Tuhoe.

5

Drenched and hanging tutu
the flimsier foliage smashed
by heavy snow, poor wronged rainforest.
Birds rattle and cough
sneeze out whistles and bells

mares' tails wipe the sky, wind's getting up
deepens green the darkening lake
closing down for night
the green of the deep still lake
still water   after the sun has gone.

REIHANA ROBINSON

On Our Knees or Homage to the Potato

In war zones agriculture is the first casualty
The enemy must be made hungry
You read stories about how she fed her family on grass
Boiling water with a strand of herb, a strip of bark
How good one raspberry served on a leaf
How good

The potato's true worth
Prances onto the stage in groggy
Sleep-deprived dirty glory

Da-da
Here I am
Je suis ici
I am here

On our knees sheltering from a storm of bullets
Begging lusting
Oh God of Potato teach us this gratitude
Now

BILL MANHIRE
Hotel Emergencies

The fire alarm sound: is given as a howling sound. Do not use
  the lifts. The optimism sound: is given as the sound of a man
  brushing his teeth. Do not go to bed. The respectability sound: is
  given as a familiar honking sound. Do not run, do not sing. The
  dearly-departed sound: is given as a rumble in the bones. Do not
  enter the coffin. The afterlife sound: is given as the music of the
  spheres. It will not reconstruct. The bordello sound: is given as
  a small child screaming. Do not turn on the light. The accident
  sound: is given as an ambulance sound. You can hear it coming
  closer, do not crowd the footpaths. The execution sound: is given
  as the sound of prayer. Oh be cautious, do not stand too near

or you will surely hear: the machinegun sound, the weeping mother
  sound, the agony sound, the dying child sound: whose voice is
  already drowned by the approaching helicopter sound: which is
  given as the dead flower sound, the warlord sound, the hunting
  and fleeing and clattering sound, the amputation sound, the
  bloodbath sound, the sound of the President quietly addressing
  his dinner; now he places his knife and fork together (a polite and
  tidy sound) before addressing the nation

and making a just and necessary war sound: which is given as a
  freedom sound (do not cherish memory): which is given as a
  security sound: which is given as a prisoner sound: which is given
  again as a war sound: which is a torture sound and a watchtower
  sound and a firing sound: which is given as a Timor sound: which
  is given as a decapitation sound (do not think you will not gasp
  tomorrow): which is given as a Darfur sound: which is given as a

Dachau sound: which is given as a dry river-bed sound, as a wind
in poplars sound: which is given again as an angry god sound:

which is here as a Muslim sound: which is here as a Christian sound:
which is here as a Jewish sound: which is here as a merciful
god sound: which is here as a praying sound: which is here as
a kneeling sound: which is here as a scripture sound: which is
here as a black-wing sound: as a dark-cloud sound: as a black-ash
sound: which is given as a howling sound: which is given as a
fire-alarm sound:

which is given late at night, calling you from your bed (do not use
the lifts): which is given as a burning sound, no, as a human
sound, as a heartbeat sound: which is given as a sound beyond
sound: which is given as the sound of many weeping: which is
given as an entirely familiar sound, a sound like no other, up
there high in the smoke above the stars.

ANNE KENNEDY
I was a feminist in the eighties

To be a feminist you need to have
a good night's sleep.

To be a feminist you need to
have your consciousness raised
and have a good night's sleep.

To be a feminist you need to
have regard for your personal well-being
and have your consciousness raised
and have a good night's sleep.

To be a feminist you need to
have a crack at financial independence
have regard for your personal well-being
have your consciousness raised
and have a good night's sleep.

To be a feminist you need to
champion women, have a crack at
financial independence, have regard
for your personal well-being
have your consciousness raised and
have a good night's sleep.

To be a feminist you need to do the
childminding, washing, shopping, cooking and cleaning
while your mind is on higher matters
and champion women, have a crack

at financial independence, have regard
for your personal well-being
have your consciousness raised
and have a good
night's sleep.

To be a feminist you need to button
your coat thoughtfully, do the childminding
washing, shopping, cooking and cleaning
while your mind is on higher matters
and champion women, have a crack at
financial independence, have regard for
your personal well-being, have your
consciousness raised and have
a good night's
sleep.

To be a feminist you need to
engage in mature dialogue with
your spouse on matters of domestic
equality, button your coat thoughtfully
do the childminding, washing, shopping, cooking and cleaning
while your mind is on higher matters
and champion women, have a crack at
financial independence, have regard
for your personal well-being, have
your consciousness raised and
have a good
night's
sleep.

Then a lion came prowling out of the jungle
and ate the feminist all up.

LYNN JENNER

When I had a son in his early teens

When I had a son in his early teens
a Russian thought formed in my head
that if a war came I would cut off
the index finger of his right hand
so that he would be no use for fighting.
The part of me which visits
hospitals would do the cutting.
I wouldn't care if he hated me
for what I did.
I might even be pleased.
By this time I knew that he was nearly
a man, and that if I didn't cut his finger off
or shoot him in the foot, he would go.
Even if he was afraid.
Even if he thought it was pointless.
Now he is a man and I ask him
to carry my suitcase.

duck

there's a duck on the road
its head sticking out of the shiny dark
twisting like a tap turned on turned off
it's hurt, it's stuck
on the thin white line that divides
four lanes of manic traffic

why did the duck cross the road?
because she thought she had to
because her mother had done it before
because she didn't think she had to think
because she was hungry

onoff onoff onoff

consider for a moment
the domestic situation of the duck:
the rough nip on the neck the bluster
the headshove under water
the fluster and wing flap indignant
the flash of an indigo armband

why did she fall for it this time?
the fat wibble wobble of a batty criss cross trundle
on the Main South Road, ten little Speights babies
left tweedling on the thick brown skin of the river

she didn't know / oh yes she did
oh no she didn't / too right she did

she knew damned well and she should have known better

onoff onoff onoff

someone's got to do something
oh yeah! she's made her bed and now she'll have to lie in it
you'd be far better off to whack her on the head
and put her out of her misery
just how much can you afford to invest in a duck anyway?

this is a classic film noir
one of us is the femme fatale
one is the chap's best friend
I just wish I could remember the ending!

I'm a gymnast on a narrow beam
I ride the slipstream of hot metal
it's wet, the road is slippery
people are in a hurry to get home
I'm a collapsing Z

I grab the duck

    the twiggy cretonne feathers scissorslip
    a bit I dig harder into her hot gut the way
    I would if I was stuffing her before basting

I wrench her off the road

    dumb demure dappling   her neck wobbling
    away from me   her open beak   her dribble

I hold up the duck like a trophy

WOMAN KILLED IN RUSH HOUR TRAFFIC
SHE WAS TAKING HER LIFE IN HER HANDS
SHE WAS HOLDING A DUCK IN HER HANDS
SHE WAS OLD ENOUGH TO KNOW BETTER

all the way home I crash the gears crying
and I rush into the house to get a blanket
and the others say what's wrong
and I say I've got a runover duck in the car
and I need a blanket and they all start to laugh
and make helpful suggestions like

it won't make any difference
I've got more to worry about than a bloody duck
it'll be dead by now anyway and there's no room
left in the garden to bury things, god almighty,
we've already got two dogs, three mice, five goldfish
and the rabbit buried there, what more do you want?

and they're right of course
when I go back out to bring her in
she's dead

aue! aue! what will I do with you, *my own aisling?*

Queen of Spades in a brown tweed coat,
rock skimmer in scungy water, corky decoy,
topsy turvy lady of dibble and dabble, mud shoveller,
funny puddler, silly quack quack

JANET FRAME
Yet Another Poem About a Dying Child

Poets and parents say he cannot die
so young, so tied to trees and stars.
Their word across his mouth obscures
and cures his murmuring good-bye.
He babbles, *they say*, of spring flowers,

who for six months has lain
his flesh at a touch bruised violet,
his face pale, his hate clearer
than milky love that would smooth over
the pebbles of diseased bone.

Pain spangles him like the sun,
He cries and cannot say why.
His blood blossoms like a pear tree.
He does not want to eat or keep
its ugly windfall fruit.

He does not want to spend or share
the engraved penny of light
that birth put in his hand
telling him to hold it tight.
Will parents and poets not understand?

He must sleep, rocking the web of pain
till the kind furred spider will come
with the night-lamp eyes and soft tread
to wrap him warm and carry him home
to a dark place, and eat him.

LYNN DAVIDSON
How to live by the sea

Be like the terns crouched on the shore.
Still under an empty sky.

Stake your life on warnings.
The gulls will circle, shrieking, before rain.

Keep one craft at hand.
A kayak out back among nasturtiums.

Walk lightly.
The grey heron will haunt your letterbox.

Cultivate patience.
The orca may pass by here again.

Settle for disorder.
All summer you will swim before you wake.

MEG CAMPBELL
Silly

I am stepping over the dogs to reach you
in the kitchen. While your back's turned
I'll grip you in my arms (which are like
the legs of a jumping spider). When you
turn and fend me off, shoo-ing me
to a safe distance, you purse your lips
for a kiss, and "THAT'S THAT!" you snap.
"IT'S LOVE!" I think. One day
I'll swing you over my head
on to the bed, and steal twenty dollars
from your wallet, and sit on you
until you cry "MERCY" and
"I LOVE YOU WITH THE LOVE
OF A JUMPING SPIDER" which is hard
and shiny, and I'll step backwards on to
the dogs, who'll shriek, and we'll be
united in soothing their feelings.
Why is it so sweet to me — you
in the kitchen, and me at arm's length?
Silly.

KATE CAMP

Snow White's Coffin

Tom Waits records the sound of frying chicken
that's how he achieves his pops and crackles.
Our old unit had a hooked grey arm,
it was a trunk of wood with woven speakers.

As a child I worried about forgetting:
The hexagonal handle, a creamy honey cell.
That flaw in the lino resembling Donald Duck
while the others of its kind looked like grey bells.

Sometimes life would seem too big, even then
an empty Sunday where you drifted as a ghost.
I saw *Bonnie and Clyde* on such a day,
as I recall, in black and white

when the bullets came
they died like oceans
full of slow turbulence
as if brought by death to life.

Why preserve one's childhood memories?
So, like Egyptians, they might be packed into the grave?
That I would sit up nights, eating from the Haworth mug
spoonfuls of plain sugar mixed with cinnamon.

Is there room in the sarcophagus for that,
for the feeling of the covers of paperbacks,
in which girls survive, among great trees,
girls who make mistakes in forests.

One thing I loved was to pick the scabs on my knees
while sitting on the toilet.
Do I need to say, I ate them?
Who is taking this down?

~

The Dutch I believe, have built a car one molecule long.
I've seen its silly form, its atom wheels.
It looks nothing like a car, it looks to be a pupa
some kind of baby bee surprised by disaster in its cell.

The problems of this world will not be solved by tiny cars.
Everything is small enough already
and there is too much, too much of everyone.
To understand your life you need another whole life.

I think we are sitting here on the axis my friend
that is why we feel a bit unwell.
Buried in us are minutes, days, mornings slept late
nights of no rest, turning to one side

turning again like a tide
sweating into the bodies of hot beds
those bucketfuls of moisture.
I think that futures might be in us too

driving in tiny cars, they are opening their minute glove
boxes and with infinitesimal hands
draw out maps too small to imagine
but they imagine them, they look at the lists of streets

all arranged according to the alphabet.
And then I think they throw the book away.
And they get out from the car
and they throw the keys into the ocean

howling. They do not want to go to places in books.
They will not drive
in their molecule cars
those ridiculous cartoons.

~

Snow White's Coffin
is an integrated radio and record player
that introduced Plexiglas to the domestic interior.
Relieve yourself of the excruciating clutter of the world

is what it says to you
everything you thought was *being alive*
is revealed as a problem
which can be solved by good design.

JAMES BROWN

No Rest

Wake up facing wall.
Sound of rain battering roof.
Taste of cabbage in mouth.
Fall of limbs into clothes.
No milk.
No bread.
No power to fridge.
Grin of spider in bath.
Smell of cat shit in shower.
Laughter of empty coat hook.
Recall coat on work chair back.
Sprint down floundering road.
Battering of rain on head.
Battering of rain on world.
Battering of hand on departing bus.
Arrival of traction engine.
Driver in no hurry due to battering rain.
War and Peace passed among passengers.
Battering of rain on eventual arrival.
Swipe entry to building.
Swipe entry to building.
Brush teeth with finger.
Cement smile to face.
Make wet joke to silent room.
Assume desk.
Spill tea.
Log-in "rejected."
Work "unable to be retrieved."
Gaze at computer with libelous intent.

Called into boss for chat.

Hurried pulling up of socks.

Told to pick up pace.

Told to wake up ideas.

Told to pull up socks.

Resume desk.

Leave message with IT.

Try to hang up phone.

Try to pick up pieces.

Try to not cry.

Take stock.

Take deep breath.

Take running jump.

Thump computer.

Thump printer.

Thump stapler.

Thumb stapled to work station.

Stagger to sickbay.

Told to lose weight.

Told to gain confidence.

Told to relax.

Walk carefully to tearoom.

Make weak tea joke to back of queue.

Coincide with boss.

Smile through clenched toes.

Resume desk.

Leave message with IT.

Tip tea in pot plant.

Try to avoid meeting.

Try to avoid trouble.

Try to avoid void.

Seep of seconds into lunch hour.

Exit building via disused stairwell.

Coincide with boss.

Smile through clenched silence.

Eat scalding pie in rain-strewn doorway.

Eat scalding fingers in rain-strewn pie.

Eat strewn words in rain-scalded head.

Resume desk.

Leave message with IT.

Traipse into rudderless meeting.

Tapping of rain on window.

Tapping of finger on pen.

Tapping of words on brain.

Shake head.

Nod head.

Nod off.

Wake to posture sliding from chair.

Wake to improbable dreams involving team leader.

Wake to startling new punchline to Noddy joke.

Strive to ignore buzzing fluoro.

Strive to think of sensible question.

Strive not to tell Noddy joke.

Agree to differ.

Agree to compromise.

Agree to agree.

File out into endless corridor.

Resume desk.

Leave message with IT.

Visit toilet.

Coincide with boss.

Smile through clenched bottom.

Resume desk.

Draft dazzling letter of resignation.

Visit recycling bin.

Make small talk with stressed colleagues.

Make molehill out of mountain.

Make dart.

Resume desk.

Stick pin in desk mascot.

Look busy.

Look out of window.

Look into lost soul.

Leave message with IT.

Attempt work in hardcopy.

Work hard at copy attempt.

Copy attempt at work hard.

Ingest fumes from correction fluid.

Experience time as gelid ellipse.

Drip wobble of seconds into stupendous bullet points:

- Literacy practice is effective when it leads to
  improved literacy achievement
- Teacher efficacy is strongly related
  to being an effective teacher
- The poem is about the mind's ability
  to fashion for itself a series of problems
  and thereby a series of possible solutions
- God is always greater than all our troubles

Find lost lucky penny.

Shut down computer.

Ha fucking ha.

Sprint down exit stairwell.

Forget coat.

Forget to buy milk.

Forget to learn from mistakes.

Catch world's most missable bus.

Crawl of nose against window.

Crawl of babies into adulthood.

Crawl of snails into advanced species.

Battering of rain on bus.

Battering of rain on suburbs.

Battering of rain on rain.

Sprint up floundering road.

Collect sodden demands from letterbox.

Climb 4,000 steps to front door.

Stare at key through locked window.

Contort back through stuffed toilet louvres.

Seek illumination from 40 watt bulb.

Seek sustenance from reheated dinner.

Seek picture in snow on telly.

Try to make bed to lie in.

Try to make light of day.

Try to make light of darkness.

JENNY BORNHOLDT
Wedding Song

Now you are married
try to love the world
as much as you love
each other. Greet it as your husband,
wife. Love it with all your
might as you sleep
breathing against its back.

Love the world, when, late at night,
you come home to find snails
stuck to the side of the house
like decoration.

Love your neighbours.
The red berries on their trampoline
their green wheelbarrow.

Love the man walking on
water, the man up a
mast. Love the light moving
across the Island Princess.

Love your grandmother when she tells you
her hair is three-quarters "cafe au lait."

Try to love the world, even when you discover
there is no such thing as *The Author*
any more.

Love the world, praise
god, even, when your aerobics instructor
is silent.

Try very hard to love
your mailman, even though he regularly
delivers you Benedicto Clemente's mail.

Love the weta you find on the path,
injured by alteration.

Love the tired men, the burnt
house, the handlebars of light
on the ceiling.

Love the man on the bus who says
it all amounts to a fishing rod
or a light bulb.

Love the world of the garden.
The keyhole of bright green grass
where the stubborn palm
used to be,
bees so drunk on ginger flowers
that they think the hose water
is rain
your hair tangled in heartsease.

Love the way,
when you come inside,
insects find their way out
from the temporary rooms of
your clothes.

TUSIATA AVIA
Wild Dogs Under My Skirt

I want to tattoo my legs.
Not blue or green
but black.

I want to sit opposite the tufuga
and know he means me pain.
I want him to bring out his chisel
and hammer
and strike my thighs
the whole circumference of them
like walking right round the world
like paddling across the whole Pacific
in a log
knowing that once you've pushed off
loaded the dogs on board
there's no looking back now, Bingo.

I want my legs as sharp as dogs' teeth
wild dogs
wild Samoan dogs
the mangy kind that bite strangers.

I want my legs like octopus
black octopus
that catch rats and eat them.

I even want my legs like centipedes
the black ones
that sting and swell for weeks.

And when it's done
I want the tufuga
to sit back and know they're not his
they never were.

I want to frighten my lovers
let them sit across from me
and whistle through their teeth.

COMMANDER
MODUZA PROCRIS

INDIA

CURATED BY SUDEEP SEN

COMMON LASCAR
PANTOPORIA HORDONIA

AMIT CHAUDHURI

The Writers

(On constantly mishearing "rioting" as "writing" on the BBC)

There has been writing for ten days now,
unabated. People are anxious, fed up.
There is writing in Paris, in disaffected suburbs,
but also in small towns, and old ones like Lyon.
The writers have been burning cars; they've thrown
homemade Molotov cocktails at policemen.
Contrary to initial reports, the writers
belong to several communities: Algerian
and Caribbean, certainly, but also Romanian,
Polish, and even French. Some are incredibly
young: the youngest is thirteen.
They stand edgily on street-corners, hardly
looking at each other. Long-standing neglect
and an absence of both authority and employment
have led to what are now ten nights of writing.

AMIT CHAUDHURI

Insomniac

There is that crack of light
which becomes clearer after a few moments.
Though you shut your eyes
that clarity neither develops nor changes.
Then you move in and out
with your breathing.
And, not sleep, but a whole universe comes to you,
newsprint, an unfair observation,
the twilight of characters.
Until even that fades
and you are left with the spaces it occupied,
the false, heavy calm of waiting,
and, that crack of light,
now become mortal, become vulnerable,
announces to you the safety and comfort of what is to come.

Postmortem

The nurse left work at five o'clock.

She had seen the dead woman's husband sitting, near the entrance, under the yellow sign that Doctor Ahmed had hung some months ago. "While You Wait, Meditate." He was sitting with his arms crossed, elbows cupped in the palms of his hands, and hadn't looked up when she passed him on her way out.

Just after lunch, a convoy had come from the Army camp. Two uniformed soldiers carried in the body on a stretcher. One soldier, a small rifle in his left hand, threw open the office door and announced the Colonel. Doctor Ahmed had automatically stood up.

The Colonel was plump. He looked calm and extremely clean, the way bullfrogs do, gleaming green and gold in the mud. He put his baton on the table and asked the nurse to leave the office.

When Doctor Ahmed rang his bell, the nurse went back in and was told to get his wife, Zakia, from their home on the top floor. Usually, he just called her on the phone. The nurse hurried up, guessing that she was also to give the news about the Colonel.

Doctor Zakia was a pediatrician but she immediately understood why she was to do the postmortem. The soldiers put the stretcher in the operating room and left. The doctor removed the white sheet and then, choking, recited the Fatiha. It was difficult for her to continue the examination — she had a grown-up daughter.

Then the nurse was alone with the young woman for over four hours, cleaning her of the blood and the filth, and then stitching her up. The abdomen and thighs had turned green, but this was expected. There was a pronounced swelling of the tongue and lips.

The nurse wondered whether the body would last till the funeral. If there was a protest, it would take the entire day in the sun for the procession to reach the cemetery.

A year ago, a doctor in the north had announced that the corpse brought to him was of a woman who had been gang-raped. This was a mistake. The Army put out the story that the woman used to come to the camp for customers and that her husband found out and had probably got her killed.

In the warm and stuffy room, the nurse realized that her teeth were chattering. She stopped and for a long while stared at the back of her gloved hands. Then she turned them over, as if she were praying, and studied the film of dark coagulated matter on her fingers.

There was no slippage and still it was hard work. Doctor Zakia would probably tell the family that the body had been washed thrice. The women would nevertheless insist on doing what was proper. How was she to save them? No one teaches you in nursing school to cover cigarette burns on the privates or to stitch torn nipples.

When she finally stepped out of the room she was startled to see a dozen soldiers in the hallway. She met the eye of the one closest to her and flinched, but he was quiet, even shy, like a dog that has brought in a squirrel and dropped it on the carpet.

At six, she was sitting in front of the television in her tiny living room. And there she was, the young woman in her wedding photograph. The newsreader said the body had been found in a ditch after the woman had gone missing for twenty-six hours. She had been struck sometime at night by a speeding vehicle.

AMITAVA KUMAR
Milk Is Good For You

The boy is barely seven. He tells his teacher that if he looks long enough at the sun, he can make his sight go black. His teacher slaps him on the head, not with force, but still it stings, and the boy smiles.

He is a good boy. The teacher has known him since he was a baby. The boy's father is the teacher's first cousin; he is also older than the teacher by at least ten years, and has been the village-tailor for as long as he can remember.

Once, when the boy was four, he was peeing in the teacher's front yard and announced that he was going to start drinking more milk because his pee was coming out yellow.

Milk?

"Yes," the boy said, "milk is good for you and can make your pee white again."

A little over two years later, the teacher had started the geography class in the afternoon when someone brought the news of the explosion. They raced to the hospital on his bicycle, the boy sitting behind him on the carriage, the small hands clutching his teacher's shirt. In the waiting room, he noticed that the child had peed in his pants.

The boy's elder brother was inside. He had stepped into a millet field three miles north, where the Army had planted mines and marked with a red strip of cloth and a painted sign. Doctor

Ahmed tried his best. He stitched the injured leg but was unable to save an arm.

Before the summer was over, the older boy dropped out and began to work in the tea-shop at the bus-station. He was a hard worker. You can see him there at all hours of the day, working with his one good arm, boiling the milky mixture till the dark tea-leaves rise to the top looking like dead ants.

The younger one still comes to school. He is clever. Just the other day in class he collected the snow from the windowsill and asked if they could sell it in packets in other parts of the country where it is hot.

The teacher later repeated this story at the tea-shop. A customer joked, "Maybe the Army can help with that. Their trucks can take the snow back to the plains." The one-armed boy looked up from the kerosene stove. He said, "Or the snow could be used in the coffins in which we could send back all the soldiers."

ARUNDHATHI SUBRAMANIAM

Epigrams for Life After Forty

Between the doorbell
and the death knell
is the tax exemption certificate.

There are fewer capital letters
than we supposed.

Other people's stories will do.
Sticky nougatine green-and-pink stories.
Other people's stories.

Untenanting is more difficult
than unbelonging.

The body? The same alignment
of flesh, bone, the scent of soap, yesterday's
headlines, a soupçon of opera.

But there are choices
other than cringing vassal state
and walled medieval town.

And there is a language
of aftermath,
a language of ocean and fluttering sail,
of fishing villages malabared
by palm, and dreams laced
with arrack and moonlight.

And it can even be
enough.

ARUNDHATHI SUBRAMANIAM

How Some Hindus Find Their Personal Gods

(for A.S., who wonders about ishta devtas)

It's about learning to trust
the tug
that draws you to a shadowed alcove
in your life
undisturbed by footfall
and butter lamps

a blue dark coolness
where you find him
waiting patiently
that perfect minor deity —

shy, crumbly,
oven-fresh, just a little
wry, content to play a cameo
in everyone's life but your own.

A god who looks
like he could understand
errors in translation
blizzards on the screen
lapses in memory

who might even learn by rote
the fury
the wheeze
the Pali,
the pidgin,
the gnashing mixer-grinder

the awkward Remington stutter
of your heart,
who could make them his own.

After that you can settle for none other.

MICHELLE CAHILL
The Piano Lesson

My hands are stricken. Do they not brush your sleeve?
Are they not stripped by this embrace? Such brevity:
light aslant on the maple, flooding us with its promise,
as if there were things outside our selves, or our words.

There are cities whose landscapes we chart. How dry
the river seems as dusk blanches. I twist in your arms,
where my aches and stings are electric. Your hammers
strike my strings, then rest, until the sound uncouples.

You have spent epistolary days rehearsing a solitary
composition; variations on the same étude to balance
what you have abandoned for loveliness. No exception
to this, I fasten my bra as you lie, perfectly naked.

There's no indignity. I think we're saved by the purple
darkness. I return to the street, unable to disguise a flush
in my cheeks. Absorbed by stilettos, subways, the slow
traffic, for a few hours, I feel immortal as any fugitive.

What bitter chords should I wait for? I forget to ask.
You have tried to get behind all the music this world
makes. My hands are stricken by the lustre of ebony
at my keyboard. Now I work. Play the silent harmonics.

MICHELLE CAHILL
Kālī from Abroad

Kālī, you are the poster-goddess, sticking out your black
tongue like Gene Simmons from Kiss, a kick in the teeth,
with your punk-blue leggings, your skull and scissor charms.

You swing a trident, a demon's head and dance on the bones
of a pale Shiva. I recall the convincing eyes of a girl cripple
carrying your bottled effigy as our bus careened to a dusty halt.

Some say you morphed from Pārvatī, drunk on blood,
others cite your superhero leap from Durgā's brow to slay
the self-cloning serpent before a Haka dance on mythic soil.

By a hundred Sanskrit names, India claims you in a single text,
while in *Zen and the Art of Motorcycle Maintenance*, you are
"the grass and the dew," on screen, our contemporary Judge Judy

having a bad hair day. I'd argue for your cosmopolitanism,
a global denizen, you're adroit in drugs and aphrodisiacs, a nude
dominatrix, a feminist export with a sadomasochistic bent.

A figure of partition you were cover girl for *Time* magazine.
A neo-pagan diva, your wholeness is darkness fashioned
from light, moon-breasted, with eyes of fire, with Brahmā's feet,

Varuna's watery thighs. You rise from the grave, step over
carnage, feeding the world and your severed self with blood.
Stripped bare as Duchamp's Bride, you set Bachelors in motion.

PRISCILA UPPAL

Identity Crisis

My cat thinks it's a dog.

My dog thinks it's a horse.

My horse thinks it's a car.

My car thinks it's a train.

My train thinks it's a submarine.

My submarine thinks it's a skyscraper.

My skyscraper thinks it's a museum.

My museum thinks it's a carnival.

My carnival thinks it's a funeral.

My funeral thinks it's a birth.

My birth thinks it's an episode.

My episode thinks it's eternal.

My eternal thinks it's hope.

My hope thinks it's cynicism.

My cynicism thinks it's time.

My time thinks it's anachronism.

My anachronism thinks it's pride.

My pride thinks it's a cat.

PRISCILA UPPAL
Books Do Hold Me at Night

As I open my eyes in the morning, so do books.
Eat breakfast, lunch, dinner and dessert at my side.
Amuse on subways, trains, and planes.
Hold my tongue in meetings and during the news.
Take my temperature when I'm feverish.
Mourn when I'm sad.

I've had orgasms with books, alone and in unison.
Travelled to the ends of the earth.
Teetered on the edge of pools and baths.
Waited patiently in cafés for my safe return.
Stayed tight to the chest in the dark.

Books dressed me during puberty.
Held their own at university.
Knew before I did that *he* and *he* and *she* were not the one.
Stood quietly aside while my babies were born.
Sometimes beat me senseless.

Books sweat with me on the elliptical.
Idle on summer porches.
Recognize my neighbours, and crawl
into my children's hands.
Sing on birthdays, and treasure old memories more
fondly than I do.

Change hats: father to uncle, daughter to professor.
Books are survivors.
Harness the crowd. Rewire the individual.

Know when to hit the brakes, when to risk it off the cliff.
I even believe, though you insist otherwise, that you know
how to die.

And now that we're on the subject.
My most loyal companions, I leave you
all my worldly and unworldly possessions.
Don't let me down. Beware of fire.
Please, do something grand.

PRIYA SARUKKAI CHABRIA

Everyday Things in My Life

I

I'll meet you here.[1] In the meantime I check the mail, call the
booksellers, iron clothes dowsed in yesterday's breeze and consume
cups of jasmine tea. Sunlight slides down the far wall and eddies
across the floor to lap around the ancient walnut wood desk near
the windows; the wine-red Persian carpet with its central shamsa
sunburst medallion and borders of neat diamonds grows dimmer
underfoot. I will await you; I will wait long past the rush hour, even
though the sun has crossed over to the other side of the house and
readies to slide into tomorrow between a tangle of trees and far
buildings and then curve beneath them.[2] I shall wait till lights come
on in the buildings, and until they are turned off. If you do not come,
I shall say it does not matter. You could believe this.[3]

---

1. field at the edge of the Milky Way: brilliance behind, black vastness ahead, at
the rim, wheeling galaxies
2. *"What if I say I am you.?"* ibid, p.154
3. . . . though the adult heart is usually about five inches in length, three and a
half inches in breadth at its broadest and two and a half inches in thickness.
However, the organ is extremely sturdy, beating without a break from its
formation in the womb until death. The glistening appearance of its inner
surface is due to the transparent endocardium membrane. Wounds of the
heart are often immediately fatal, but not necessarily so. They may be non-
penetrating, when death may occur from hemorrhage, or subsequently from
pericarditis, or on the other hand, the patient may recover.

2

Sometimes light wants to clutch whatever it can:[4]
space, as it falls through, igniting it like a cloud from within
as if in an act of visual echolalia while in
the softening dusk that grows from earth upwards
beyond trees-buildings-clouds-sky
something, not a leaf, falls like a leaf.[5]
and something unheard gargles like an inky fountain[6]
and someone living prays to give up the dead[7]
and fails.

---

4. George Szirtes
5. Derek Walcott
6. Bao Jing
7. " . . . *veils of such transparency blew across her face that she no longer knew what she was seeing . . .*" ibid, p. 260

3

Ap	ple,	pear,	man	go:
He	cuts	fruits	for	me.
I	make	him	daal	rice.
To	get	her,	read	books.
How	man	y	more	days
Are	we	thus	gift	ed?

4

A vase of flowers squats in sunlight.[8] On the sideboard, a bowl of fruit. Above it, branches reflect in the mirror's bright rectangle. On the polished wood[9] of the dining table I lay mats, plates, cutlery, napkins. Pour a thick stream of water into a crystal decanter cut with diamond designs; it is an object of great beauty that cannot be replaced. Each time I touch it, my heart beats a little faster. Curiously, the water looks heavier with sunlight streaming through.

---

8. whales beached on the white continent as far as the eye can see: stormclouds swept up from the ocean, lumpy, dark, lying on their sides, not gasping. Like elephants that seek out secret cavernous graveyards to die in, their ivory yellowing like dusty tallow, ribcages like broken teeth, the whales swim here, onto this melting shore of ice led by their song; they beguile themselves, become their own sirens, become liquefying moonstone.
9. Voyager has proved beyond doubt that storms the size of Earth rage on the surface of Jupiter. Winds reach speeds of 15,000 miles per hour. The sun is too far away to cause these effects; therefore Jupiter's storms are caused by something else.

5

As I wait, I scan a questionnaire sent by a literary journal. Their last issue was a Special on terror to which I contributed; now this. Does terror affect my daily life? What do I deem as terror? Did . . . I close the page and browse. The bell rings. A couriered package smudged with a scrawl and foreign stamps.[10] Inside, a book of poems of the rarest elegance, rigour and luminosity.[11] D has kept his word.

I return to the room. A pair of pigeons, startled, flies towards the window, their smooth shapes becoming oval flurries as they thrash wings, pppada-ppaada-ddaa-daaa against partially closed panes before escaping. On the slim marble of the windowsill, curls of down, grey on veined white, which I blow out. Should I leave the room, the pair will return to roost amid bookshelves. They never learn.

---

10. . . . under skies of cracked crystal, plum wine trapped in its veins, darkening the fractured dome, spins a mirror that captures those who look into it and reflects to each an identity they as yet do not know, but which exists in their future or their past; what is more, this is an identity they will meet. [LR]
11. for it is well known that people can transform from hatred to forgiveness for no apparent reason as is frequently witnessed in survivors from war zones: having lost everyone and everything such people become apostles of peace and love. Ref: Amazon, Gaza, Kashmir, etc.
"*. . . the sparkle in a drop of dew is sieved through dawn so all that remains is sparkle*"

6

Salammbo leans at an angle on the topmost shelf, a 1908 edition.
Repeatedly read and passed over, today, in the space of waiting,
I reach for its musty red hardcover.[12] Blow on it. Open it with
the care brought on by neglect and its tainted delicateness. Page
corners crumple on touch.[13] Dark moons, wormdrawn, burrow
through, chapter after chapter. I pluck fresh neem[14] leaves and
place their acrid scent between pages to drive away silverfish.

---

12. However, certain possessions refuse to be tattooed into a particular time,
or a specific space, such things do not abide by the rules. Rapture is foremost
amongst these: it rises unbidden at all times. Moreover, it continues to rise.
13. Drenched rapture, as in lotuses filled with rain, swollen pollen and drowned
bees.
14. . . . especially the skid of moonlight underfoot as it rolls on dew.

7

Pastry flakes on white plates. Forks gleam, sun-warmed. The wine
bottle's lengthening shadow pauses[15] as I drowsily blink. Distant
laughter opens its eyes, then snoozes.[16] I reach for your hand and
place it against my face; it fits exactly, curving like mango flesh
around its seed. Knowing you are nearby, I drift into sleep. I return
to the dream that I constantly dream these days, that dream whose
meaning I know but cannot share because my words are also only
of this world.[17]

---

15. . . . for, between the dissolution (pralaya) of the universe and the beginning
(sargam) of the next one is a pause of complete equipoise, one of "pure duration"
as time has not yet come into existence.

16.

17. The translation and significance of this stanza does not seem certain to me
but is possibly worth investigating.

SANDEEP PARMAR

Counsel

(for Anna Smaill)

Looking to ward off danger, I browse the eighth floor of the Bobst Library
      for some composite rite,
a wrist-length of red thread,
      éblouissements to blind intervening shadows.

~

    It is good luck to dream of your wedding day,
    to feed a cat from an old shoe (so long as the cat does not sneeze).
    Do not marry a man born in the same month as you,
    or eat while dressing. Tear your veil (at the altar by accident).
    Wear earrings. Not pearls. Carry salt. Drink water.

    Beware a woman carrying an empty bucket.
    Turn away from the mothers of stillborn sons, monks, pigs and lizards.
    Under no circumstances should you marry on a Tuesday. Or Thursday.
    And once you start from home, don't dare to look back.

~

How to coin the finest and most singular antidote —
to dance against possible risk?

From PR6003.U64 —
the fair-weather lesbians of Dorothy Bussy's *Olivia* —
to *The Diary of Virginia Woolf: 1915–1919* [PR6045.072]

we plunge straight into Lily the "simple-hearted" servant, her indiscretions.
A married Miss Stephen keeps schtum
in her tremorous florals two sizes too big.

Zigzagging to PR4863.A33 *The Letters of Charles and Mary Lamb*:
"Your goose found her way into our larder with infinite discretion.
Judging by her Giblets which we have sacrificed first,
    she is a most sensible Bird."
[C. L. to John Rickman, 30 December 1816]

At PR4231.A43: *Robert Browning and Elizabeth Barrett: the courtship correspondence* —
Nuances of love and outrage elongate a shortened life.
I drift towards one leaning oversize *Wandering of the Soul* [PJ1551.E3];
Egyptian Papyri transmuted into spells for safe passage in the afterlife.
"Do not stop to play draughts with the Dead
lest you be trapped for eternity."

To the Brothers Grimm [PT921.K56] —
Three women turned into identical flowers in a field.
Only one returned home every night. At dawn she said to her husband:
"If you come this morning and pick me,
I shall be set free and stay with you forever."
Imperative chance. He chose correctly.

~

Dearest one, the riddle of marriage admits no luck.
What it recognises is pure —
it fires the dew from sleeping grasses.

Only know that he will not err (and nor will you) where love
has paused in an evening's silence to light the unlit road.

SANDEEP PARMAR
Invocation

To be of use, but nothing will decant. Perilous consonant, seized as jewel, betrothed as fire is to the ordinary. A spell; a note. Combatant of will and engraver of sighs. Poultice to the hush, to the whispers of women in corded rooms and to the glows beneath doorways. Purchaser of anointments, slatherer of knives and spoons. Rind of merciless ends and clothier of borrowed aliases. Trenchant penurist, hoarder of silvered lakes. Post chaise bending on the whim of royal deliverance. Coin to whom there is no weight to match the fruit of emptied forest. Animal to cistern, face to coda, god to neither me to neither them, to she. To whom one is infinitely married, and yet cannot be affixed. Enter. All that spills over from my able palm is you.

VIKRAM SETH

Sampati

"Why
do
you
cry?"
"I
flew
too
high.
Un-
done,
all
see
me
fall."

VIKRAM SETH
For Philippe Honoré

Perhaps this could have stayed unstated.
Had our words turned to other things
In the grey park, the rain abated,
Life would have quickened other strings.
I list your gifts in this creation:
Pen, paper, ink and inspiration,
Peace to the heart with touch or word,
Ease to the soul with note and chord.

How did that walk, those winter hours,
Occasion this? No lightning came;
Nor did I sense, when touched by flame,
Our story lit with borrowed powers —
Rather, by what our spirits burned,
Embered in words, to us returned.

CLOUDED YELLOW
PAPILIO HYALE

CANADA

CURATED BY TODD SWIFT

EASTERN TAILED BLUE
CUPIDO COMYNTAS

MARGARET ATWOOD

Death of a Young Son by Drowning

He, who navigated with success
the dangerous river of his own birth
once more set forth

on a voyage of discovery
into the land I floated on
but could not touch to claim.

His feet slid on the bank,
the currents took him;
he swirled with ice and trees in the swollen water

and plunged into distant regions,
his head a bathysphere;
through his eyes' thin glass bubbles

he looked out, reckless adventurer
on a landscape stranger than Uranus
we have all been to and some remember.

There was an accident; the air locked,
he was hung in the river like a heart.
They retrieved the swamped body,

cairn of my plans and future charts,
with poles and hooks
from among the nudging logs.

It was spring, the sun kept shining, the new grass

leapt to solidity;
my hands glistened with details.

After the long trip I was tired of waves.
My foot hit rock. The dreamed sails
collapsed, ragged.

    I planted him in this country
    like a flag.

Snow

Nobody stuffs the world in at your eyes.
The optic heart must venture: a jail-break
And re-creation. Sedges and wild rice
Chase rivery pewter. The astonished cinders quake
With rhizomes. All ways through the electric air
Trundle candy-bright discs; they are desolate
Toys if the soul's gates seal, and cannot bear,
Must shudder under, creation's unseen freight.
But soft, there is snow's legend: colour of mourning
Along the yellow Yangtze where the wheel
Spins an indifferent stasis that's death's warning.
Asters of tumbled quietness reveal
Their petals. Suffering this starry blur
The rest may ring your change, sad listener.

CHRISTIAN BÖK
from Eunoia

from Chapter A
(for Hans Arp)

Awkward grammar appals a craftsman. A Dada bard as daft as Tzara damns stagnant art and scrawls an alpha (a slapdash arc and a backward zag) that mars all stanzas and jams all ballads (what a scandal). A madcap vandal crafts a small black ankh — a hand-stamp that can stamp a wax pad and at last plant a mark that sparks an *ars magna* (an abstract art that charts a phrasal anagram). A pagan skald chants a dark saga (a Mahabharata), as a papal cabal blackballs all annals and tracts, all dramas and psalms: Kant and Kafka, Marx and Marat. A law as harsh as a *fatwa* bans all paragraphs that lack an A as a standard hallmark . . .

from Chapter E
(for René Crevel)

Enfettered, these sentences repress free speech. The text deletes selected letters. We see the revered exegete reject metred verse: the sestet, the tercet — even *les scènes élevées en grec*. He rebels. He sets new precedents. He lets cleverness exceed decent levels. He eschews the esteemed genres, the expected themes — even *les belles lettres en vers*. He prefers the perverse French esthetes: Verne, Péret, Genet, Perec — hence, he pens fervent screeds, then enters the street, where he sells these letterpress newsletters, three cents per sheet. He engenders perfect newness wherever we need fresh terms . . .

from Chapter I

(for Dick Higgins)

Writing is inhibiting. Sighing, I sit, scribbling in ink this pidgin script. I sing with nihilistic witticism, disciplining signs with trifling gimmicks — impish hijinks which highlight stick sigils. Isn't it glib? Isn't it chic? I fit childish insights within rigid limits, writing shtick which might instill priggish misgivings in critics blind with hindsight. I dismiss nitpicking criticism which flirts with philistinism. I bitch; I kibitz — griping whilst criticizing dimwits, sniping whilst indicting nitwits, dismissing simplistic thinking, in which philippic wit is still illicit . . .

from Chapter O

(for Yoko Ono)

Loops on bold fonts now form lots of words for books. Books form cocoons of comfort — tombs to hold bookworms. Profs from Oxford show frosh who do postdocs how to gloss works of Wordsworth. Dons who work for proctors or provosts do not fob off school to work on crosswords, nor do dons go off to dorm rooms to loll on cots. Dons go crosstown to look for bookshops known to stock lots of top-notch goods: cookbooks, workbooks — room on room of how-to books for jocks (how to jog, how to box), books on pro sports: golf or polo. Old colophons on schoolbooks from schoolrooms sport two sorts of logo: oblong whorls, rococo scrolls — both on worn morocco . . .

from Chapter U

(for Zhu Yu)

Kultur spurns Ubu — thus Ubu pulls stunts. Ubu shuns *Skulptur*: Uruk urns (plus busts), Zulu jugs (plus tusks). Ubu sculpts junk *für Kunst und Glück.* Ubu busks. Ubu drums drums, plus Ubu strums cruths (such hubbub, such ruckus): *thump, thump; thrum, thrum.* Ubu puns puns. Ubu blurts untruth: much bunkum (plus bull), much humbug (plus bunk) — but trustful schmucks trust such untruthful stuff; thus Ubu (cult guru) must bluff dumbstruck numbskulls (such chumps). Ubu mulcts surplus funds (trust funds plus slush funds). Ubu usurps much usufruct. Ubu sums up lump sums. Ubu trumps dumb luck . . .

from "The New Ennui"

> *"The tedium is the message."*
> —Darren Wershler-Henry

"Eunoia" is the shortest word in English to contain all five vowels, and the word quite literally means "beautiful thinking." *Eunoia* is a univocal lipogram, in which each chapter restricts itself to the use of a single vowel. *Eunoia* is directly inspired by the exploits of Oulipo (*l'Ouvroir de Littérature Potentielle*) — the avant-garde coterie renowned for its literary experimentation with extreme formalistic constraints. The text makes a Sisyphean spectacle of its labour, wilfully crippling its language in order to show that, even under such improbable conditions of duress, language can still express an uncanny, if not sublime, thought.

Eunoia abides by many subsidiary rules. All chapters must allude to the art of writing. All chapters must describe a culinary banquet, a prurient debauch, a pastoral tableau and a nautical voyage. All sentences must accent internal rhyme through the use of syntactical parallelism. The text must exhaust the lexicon for each vowel, citing at least 98% of the available repertoire (although a few words do go unused, despite efforts to include them: *parallax, belvedere, gingivitis, monochord* and *tumulus*). The text must minimize repetition of substantive vocabulary (so that, ideally, no word appears more than once). The letter Y is suppressed . . .

DIANA BREBNER

Port

Sometimes the tricks you learn as a child
are useful later on. When I was beaten
or raped I learned to move myself away
to a place without pain or degradation,

to stick it out and watch at a distance,
and never to vomit. I have been lucky
in joy, and have felt exultation. I have
been moved to tears and, nowadays,

I am hardly ever beside myself. I've
read that there is a science of pain
management. I think I could be an
expert. When the surgeon removed

my port, small metal disc implanted
just under the skin of my shoulder
to make delivery of chemotherapy less
painful (and which, by the way, was

never used by the tired nurses in a hurry
who could just stick an intravenous in
a good vein and get on with it), he was
doublebooked and did the procedure

during his lunch hour. I liked this man,
he spoke honestly and listened to me
but everyone has their bad days and
this was one. In the outpatient surgery

he began and I wondered, idly, why
I could feel so much, my shoulder
deadened with anaesthetic. We talked
and he worked and I said I could feel

his hands and the instruments as he
worked and he said: No you cannot.
Can. Cannot. Can. Mutual panic
as the pain increased and he knew

he was alone, had to proceed, could
not call for help and I said: OK, Listen up.
I have gone to the top of a mountain
where it is very cold, so cold I am

frozen and cannot feel, but I can see.
And way, way down at the bottom of
the mountain there you are, tending
a fire. I can see the red flames and

imagine the heat but here I am, up at
the peak, feeling nothing. He looked
at me strangely and was silent, worked
quickly and then left me, quite alone.

I waited a long time up on that
mountain but gradually the fire went
out, and he never did come back.
I got up, and walked home, was

a body but not wholly connected.
As the afternoon wore on, the cold
wore off. I began to shake: my
hands frozen, my teeth chattering. I

couldn't stop shaking and imagined
someone lost in a storm, perhaps
at sea, hoping like crazy to make
it to port, to the safe place that is

calm, and the first thing to do when
you arrive is to be sick to your
stomach, to know you have survived
but also to know that out there,

in the dark centre of destruction,
someone you loved, and had known
so well she might have been yourself
was lost, irretrievably, at sea.

GEORGE ELLIOTT CLARKE

Monologue for Selah Bringing Spring to Whylah Falls

I cry, in the vernacular, this plain manifesto,
No matter how many fishmen offer you their laps,
Or how contrary you are in the morning,
Or how your hair gleams like dark lightning,
Or how many lies the encyclopedia preserves,
Because, Selah, I won't play them parlour-seducer games —
Card tricks of chat, sleight-of-hand caresses —
Or stick my head in books. I love your raspy,
Backwoods accent, your laughter like ice breaking up!
I'd burn dictionaries to love you even once!
    Selah, I tell myself I come to Whylah Falls
To spy the river crocheted with apple blossoms,
To touch you whose hair fans in mystery,
Whose smile is Cheshire and shadow and bliss,
Whose scent is brown bread, molasses, and milk,
Whose love is Coca-Cola and rose petals
In a ship's cabin soaked in saltwater.
But my lies lie. My colleged speech ripens before you,
Becomes Negro-natural, those green, soiled words
Whose roots mingle with turnip, carrot, and squash,
Keeping philology fresh and tasty.
    You slouch and sigh that sassy, love speech,
And aroused, very aroused, I exalt
Your decisive eyes, your definitive lips,
Your thighs that'd be emboldened by childbirth,
For when you move, every line of poetry quakes,
And I inhale your perfume — ground roses,
Distilled petals, praise your blue skirt bright

Against your bare, black legs! *You won't wear stockings!*
    I'm scripting this lyric because I'm too shy
To blurt my passion for you, Selah!
My history is white wine from a charred log,
A white horse galloping in a meadow,
A dozen chicks quitting an egg carton tomb,
But also selfish, suicidal love.
I don't want that!
    Selah, I want to lie beside you
And hear you whisper this poem and giggle.
Selah, I thought this poem was finished!
Selah, I am bust right upside the head with love!

MARY DALTON

Flirrup

Fairy squalls on the water.
I'm marooned at the window,
Waiting for the fog man,
Sewing the old black veil.
The Walls of Troy on the floor.
There's Dickey just gone up
The road in a red shirt. He's
Sure not the fog man —
Traipsing along with the swagger
Of a swiler in the spring fat.
Not a feather out of him.
Now he'd be the one to have in
For a feed of fresh flippers,
A taste of my fine figgy cake.

STEVEN HEIGHTON

The Machine Gunner

I saw them. They came like ghosts out of ground-
mist, moving
over ruined earth in waves, running

no, walking, shoulder to shoulder
like a belt of bullets or like
men: tinned meat lined on a conveyor belt as the sun

exploded in thin shafts on metal
buckles, bayonets, the nodding
spires of helmets. I heard faint battle cries

and whistles, piercing through the shriek
of fire and iron falling, the slurred
cadence of big guns. As they funneled

like a file of mourners into gaps
in the barbed wire I made quick
calculations and slipped the safety catch.

But held my fire. Alongside me
the boys in the trenches worried them with
rifles, pistols, hand grenades

but they came on, larger now, their faces
almost resolving out of hazed hot
distance, their ranks at close quarters amazing

with dumb courage, numb step, a sound of drugged
choking in gas and green mud, steaming —
Who were these men. I saw them penitent

sagging to knees. I saw their disheveled
dying. And when finally they broke
into a run it came to me

what they had always been, how I'd always,
really, seen them: boys
rushing toward us with arms

outstretched, hands clenched as if in urgent prayer,
sudden welcome or a reunion
quite unexpected. Yes. And more than this

like children, chased by something behind the lines
and hurrying to us
for rescue —

I spat and swung the gun around. Fired,
felt the metal pulse
and laid them three deep in the wire.

A. M. KLEIN

Portrait of the Poet as Landscape

I

Not an editorial-writer, bereaved with bartlett,
mourns him, the shelved Lycidas.
No actress squeezes a glycerine tear for him.
The radio broadcast lets his passing pass.
And with the police, no record. Nobody, it appears,
either under his real name or his alias,
missed him enough to report.

It is possible that he is dead, and not discovered.
It is possible that he can be found some place
in a narrow closet, like the corpse in a detective story,
standing, his eyes staring, and ready to fall on his face.
It is also possible that he is alive
and amnesiac, or mad, or in retired disgrace,
or beyond recognition lost in love.

We are sure only that from our real society
he has disappeared; he simply does not count,
except in the pullulation of vital statistics —
somebody's vote, perhaps, an anonymous taunt
of the Gallup poll, a dot in a government table —
but not felt, and certainly far from eminent —
in a shouting mob, somebody's sigh.

O, he who unrolled our culture from his scroll —
the prince's quote, the rostrum-rounding roar —

who under one name made articulate
heaven and under another the seven-circled air,
is, if he is at all, a number, an x,
a Mr. Smith in a hotel register, —
incognito, lost, lacunal.

2

The truth is he's not dead, but only ignored —
like the mirroring lenses forgotten on a brow
that shine with the guilt of their unnoticed world.
The truth is he lives among neighbours, who, though they will allow
him a passable fellow, think him eccentric, not solid,
a type that one can forgive, and for that matter, forego.

Himself he has his moods, just like a poet.
Sometimes, depressed to nadir, he will think all lost,
will see himself as throwback, relict, freak,
his mother's miscarriage, his great-grandfather's ghost,
and he will curse his quintuplet senses, and their tutors
in whom he put, as he should not have put, his trust.

Then he will remember his travels over that body —
the torso verb, the beautiful face of the noun,
and all those shaped and warm auxiliaries!
A first love it was, the recognition of his own.
Dear limbs adverbial, complexion of adjective,
dimple and dip of conjugation!

And then remember how this made a change in him
affecting for always the glow and growth of his being;
how suddenly was aware of the air, like shaken tinfoil,
of the patents of nature, the shock of belated seeing,
the loneliness peering from the eyes of crowds;
the integers of thought; the cube-roots of feeling.

Thus, zoomed to zenith, sometimes he hopes again,
and sees himself as a character, with a rehearsed role:
the Count of Monte Cristo, come for his revenges;
the unsuspected heir, with papers; the risen soul;
or the chloroformed prince awaking from his flowers;
or — deflated again — the convict on parole.

3

He is alone; yet not completely alone.
Pins on a map of a colour similar to his,
each city has one, sometimes more than one;
here, caretakers of art, in colleges;
in offices, there, with arm-bands, and green-shaded;
and there, pounding their catalogued beats in libraries, —

everywhere menial, a shadow's shadow.
And always for their egos — their outmoded art.
Thus, having lost the bevel in the ear,
they know neither up nor down, mistake the part
for the whole, curl themselves in a comma,
talk technics, make a colon their eyes. They distort —

such is the pain of their frustration — truth
to something convolute and cerebral.
How they do fear the slap of the flat of the platitude!
Now Pavlov's victims, their mouths water at bell,
the platter empty.
                          See they set twenty-one jewels
into their watches; the time they do not tell!

Some, patagonian in their own esteem,
and longing for the multiplying word,
join party and wear pins, now have a message,
an ear, and the convention-hall's regard.
Upon the knees of ventriloquists, they own,
of their dandled brightness, only the paint and board.

And some go mystical, and some go mad.
One stares at a mirror all day long, as if
to recognize himself; another courts
angels, — for here does he not fear rebuff;
and a third, alone, and sick with sex, and rapt,
doodles him symbols convex and concave.

O schizoid solitudes! O purities
curdling upon themselves! Who live for themselves,
or for each other, but for nobody else;
desire affection, private and public loves;
are friendly, and then quarrel and surmise
the secret perversions of each other's lives.

4

He suspects that something has happened, a law
been passed, a nightmare ordered. Set apart,
he finds himself, with special haircut and dress,
as on a reservation. Introvert.
He does not understand this; sad conjecture
muscles and palls thrombotic on his heart.

He thinks an impostor, having studied his personal biography,
his gestures, his moods, now has come forward to pose
in the shivering vacuums his absence leaves.
Wigged with his laurel, that other, and faked with his face,
he pats the heads of his children, pecks his wife,
and is at home, and slippered, in his house.

So he guesses at the impertinent silhouette
that talks to his phone-piece and slits open his mail.
Is it the local tycoon who for a hobby
plays poet, he so epical in steel?
The orator, making a pause? Or is that man
he who blows his flash of brass in the jittering hall?

Or is he cuckolded by the troubadour
rich and successful out of celluloid?
Or by the don who unrhymes atoms? Or
the chemist death built up? Pride, lost impostor'd pride,
it is another, another, whoever he is,
who rides where he should ride.

5

Fame, the adrenalin: to be talked about;
to be a verb; to be introduced as *The*:
to smile with endorsement from slick paper; make
caprices anecdotal; to nod to the world; to see
one's name like a song upon the marquees played;
to be forgotten with embarrassment; to be —
to be.

It has its attractions, but is not the thing;
nor is it the ape mimesis who speaks from the tree
ancestral; nor the merkin joy . . .
Rather it is stark infelicity
which stirs him from his sleep, undressed, asleep
to walk upon roofs and window-sills and defy
the gape of gravity.

6

Therefore he seeds illusions. Look, he is
the nth Adam taking a green inventory
in world but scarcely uttered, naming, praising,
the flowering fiats in the meadow, the
syllabled fur, stars aspirate, the pollen
whose sweet collision sounds eternally.
For to praise

the world — he, solitary man — is breath
to him. Until it has been praised, that part
has not been. Item by exciting item —

air to his lungs, and pressured blood to his heart. —
they are pulsated, and breathed, until they map,
not the world's, but his own body's chart!

And now in imagination he has climbed
another planet, the better to look
with single camera view upon this earth —
its total scope, and each afflated tick,
its talk, its trick, its tracklessness — and this,
this he would like to write down in a book!

To find a new function for the déclassé craft
archaic like the fletcher's; to make a new thing;
to say the word that will become sixth sense;
perhaps by necessity and indirection bring
new forms to life, anonymously, new creeds —
O, somehow pay back the daily larcenies of the lung!

These are not mean ambitions. It is already something
merely to entertain them. Meanwhile, he
makes of his status as zero a rich garland,
a halo of his anonymity,
and lives alone, and in his secret shines
like phosphorus. At the bottom of the sea.

DAVID MCGIMPSEY

In Memoriam: A. H. Jr.

A few weeks before he died
thin, thin from the cancer
Alan Hale was stopped by a teenager
who pumped gas at an L.A. station
& asked the gaunt skipper if he was alright,
if he was dieting or something
like Oprah, Lasorda or some other famous,
formerly overweighted.
"Yes that's right," the mighty sailing man said
"we're doing the series again
& this time I'm going to play Gilligan."
& he drove out into the afternoon.
Now his body is out in the Pacific
mixing with coral reef & Catalina trash,
whole with the universe, taking time out,
resting forever from the question:
who was responsible for the fate of *The Minnow*?

Brave in diagnosis, brave in chemo,
brave in goodbye. From heaven send a message,
have a few hot dogs & smile.

Once, when you were in the greenworld
tempest in the uncharted areas of the sea,
you fell under the terrible curse of Kona.
Digging through the fine island sand,
making practical refrigeration
to store Mary Ann's guava jelly
you unearthed the idol head,

its mouth downturned,
its jagged teeth poised to cut through skin.

The curse of Kona, you said
(inbetween frantic conjurings of fates
more terrible than being stranded
on an island full of idiots),
could only be cured by Watumbi's dance.
Only Watumbi's dance,
doctored to the rhythms of the tropical forest,
could deliver release into the world
of the relatively uncursed.
"Superstitions don't have to be ridiculed"
you said to Prof. Roy Hinckly PhD (TCU),
who was irreverent in answering your call
for the dance but admitted
that he had seen many things
that defy the laws of reason in his years
as a castaway in the cancerous sun.
The Professor tried his best
but couldn't help start dictating all the triumphs
his Cartesian mind had brought them all:
saved them from the deadly Mantis Carni bite
with an antidote of ground clam shells & papaya roots,
saved them from marauding Marubi headhunters
simultaneously translating their intent to kill
& finding a safe, inner-island cave
to huddle & coo about the lost USA;
saved the crew from long-term effects
of radioactive vegetables the size of trees.
The skipper set the Prof. straight, said, "son

it doesn't hurt to believe in the curse of Kona
or believe Jesus Christ is waiting for me, drunk,
on the other side; it doesn't matter tonight if I
send in a subscription for *Scientific American*,
anyway you have it we are stranded here on this island,
the two-foot hole in *The Minnow* untouched
by doctoral insight — we won't be rescued tonight."

Stupid or no, you ran around the island
through nests of damselflys, crunching
the bambooish undergrowth at your feet,
burning; sweat tracking the folds of your neck,
burning salty-dog neck & chin.
Jonas Grumby,
you ran straight into a palm tree & conked-out.
A severe case of *bumpinus on the nogginus*
but when you came to, you still believed.

You had survived the wreck
of the infamous *USS Indianapolis*;
bobbed helplessly in warm water
American canapés for swarming tiger sharks,
banjo sharks, what you will.
From Guadalcanal with your purple heart
the scars zigzagging around your shoulders
like a complex tattoo of a jungle fire.
Through the years the colors started to dull,
even in the land of Gauguin
is there ever enough tropical variety?
I don't think I can just sit back & hear anymore
not if we must touch bottom of the dolphinless sea.

Dive underneath the water
five miles deep in the Izu trench off Japan
& tell me what's there if you can.
Weren't you the leader?
There has to be a better government.

I can see the x-ray shadows.
I can see them come back after the triumph
of telling everybody you had it licked.
A shadow on the x-ray screen, a *mass*,
doctors/oncologists yapping before their knives
their cobalt, their interferon,
their understanding
there's a certain point of no return.
How did that storm come in & in 3 hours
sweep you out to sea?
Sweeping you out forever
& making you what you are?
Salut mes joyeaux naufragés.
I can see the x-ray shadows.

Monkeys throw plastic explosives overhead.
The rich couple, their money useless
still manage to have a certain
I-paid-my-way-through-Harvard kind of fun.
The Professor will work for them one day.
& Mary Ann will take to the street
to sell her preserves.
You danced with Ginger Grant,
the most beautiful woman in the world.
Her ballgown bared of its sequins,

her red hair drawn back with a beret
of sticky orchids. She rehearsed
lines from a prison movie in your ear.
You danced in the courtyard
in front of the bamboo huts
that lasted for 12 lonely years;
through typhoons, dictators & rock stars.

Japanese lanterns, crepe paper & torches
giving the cleared part of the jungle
a sense of festival & backyard safety.
The coconut-Victrola playing Paris accordion —
the air of the left lagoon bank
soft & warm, protected for the Tiki,
ready for the lost
& ever & always
nautical 260 miles SW of Honolulu.

Hours spent, beautiful, swinging imperceptibly
in a navy issue hammock,
the silhouette of your belly on the wall,
candles flickering gently on the green palm fronds,
the captain's hat over your eyes.
Skinny Mulligan, what's-his-face,
above you, ready to fall out & rake hell.
Dreams of Malaysian food, of Australian wine
of sailor stuff from Seattle to Hong Kong.
Dreams of maybe getting married,
of strolling with prams through the San Diego zoo
sort of just like I-don't-know-who.
Hours spent reading the naval manual,

(not one for staring at Manuel's navel)

tying bamboo sticks together,

sharpening bits, things for survival he says

survival enough to kill the time.

No phones, no lights, no microwave.

Hours thinking about the fate of *The Minnow*.

One wrong weather report & that was it.

It happens to everybody in some way.

Did y'all fasten your anchor

when you threw your life overboard?

"When I get back" you prayed

"I'll do my best to clear my name, extend my commission

& still surprise the world by doing something nice

for that stupid kid."

Broadway impresarios could visit the island

as much as they wanted, proposing

a musical Hamlet or a musical Lear —

it didn't help one bit.

You said "I can't remember everything, it gets lost

deep into the bright afternoons.

It's amazing, I stayed fat through it all,

through everything. Isn't that funny?"

The Skipper & Gilligan will be friends forever,

despite their tragic mistakes.

The worst things will still happen,

they always do, despite our bonds.

Things settle in the damp roots of our lungs

in the red fibres of the fibres of our muscles & rot.

It was a wild time:

sand in everything, amazing inventions.

The sputum of the atoll-gods rippling lagoon water
like spacecraft tumbling back to America.
Don't let go of my hand because I'm dying
of cancer or drowning in the Irish sea.
Brave it out & bury nothing, let it drift
with everything still wet & alive.
Let it drift aimless,
just another tour gone astray.
Christmases, rainy seasons, mosquitoes,
all forgotten, just like last February
in the suburbs.

Ces après-midis disparaissent
et Gilligan et le Capitaine goûteraient
leurs tartes aux crème d'ananas
avec nous-autres. Goodbye little buddy.

Victrola dancing Ginger accordion lighted
ricewine crepe-paper Ginger perfume
jungle Paris red-haired moonlit Ginger.
You survive, not to cry
like Pagliacci,
but because life holds to you so well.
You wore your captain's hat proudly
receiving visitors to your family restaurant:
The Skipper's Lobster Barrel
on La Cienega Blvd. in Los Angeles, California.

Dozing through a little busride
through the birch forests of Upper Canada
the tinge of diesel seeping in the luxury coach.

The view out into the stretch of winter,
faded trees scratching the horizon,
squaring out the meagre farmland.
Nothing there that wasn't frozen.
In the dark February plain
the voice of the seven stranded castaways
deep in the Boreal forest
"Skipper! Professor!"
I thought I heard somebody cry.
"I think the Howells have scurvy!"
Saying it was only a TV show
is like saying it was only a friend,
only my brother, only my father.

Put the antennae high, pay your cable bills.
To volcanoes fresh & lagoons anew.
He was like to ponder expeditious rescue.
He'd say "when I get back to civilization
I'll tell you what I'm going to do:
I'm going to have a tall glass of cold beer
& I won't spill a drop.
I'm going to order a steak, New York cut,
medium rare & two inches thick."
How thick? "Two inches thick!"
In the plate will rest the slightest residue:
blood, spice & fat
agents of flavour after the meat is gone.

JOAN MURRAY
Even the Gulls of the Cool Atlantic

The gulls of the cool Atlantic tip the foam.
The boats that warn me of fog warn me of their motion.
I have looked for my childhood among pebbles, and my home
Within the lean cupboards of Mother Hubbard and neat Albion.

A wind whose freshness blows over the cape to me
Has made me laugh at the thought of a friend whose hair is blond.
Still I laugh and place my hands across the sea
From the farthest stretch of lands to the end of the end.

I had so often run down to these shores to stare out.
If I took an island for a lover and Atlantic for my sheet,
There was no one to tell me that loving across distance would turn about
And make the here and now an elsewhere of defeat.

In my twenty-first year to have the grubby hand and slums,
Be the small child at my knee, my knee the glistening chalk
That sails to meet the stationary boat, the water sloping as it comes,
And all the Devon coast of grey and abrupt rock.

By gazing across water I have flicked many gulls from my eyes,
Shuffled small shells and green crabs to my feet.
The day is cool; the sun bright; the piper cries
Shrilly, tempering the untouched sand in delicate retreat.

Up beyond the height and over the bank, I have a friend.
How is your winter night and your summer action?
There need be little more than a teacup hour to make us both comprehend
A mature man's simplicity or grave child's sweet reaction.

RICHARD OUTRAM

Barbed Wire

Consists of two tight-twisted, separate strands
Conjoined as one: and not unlike, in fact,
Our own familiar silver wedding bands,
Though these are loosely woven, inexact,

With wide interstices, so that each makes
A circle of ellipses. Tightly caught
At random intervals, two little snakes
Of wire are crimped into a snaggled knot,

That four short ends, sharp bevel-cut, present
Unsheathed ingenious fangs. And when in place,
Stretched taut, or strewn in loose coils, may prevent
The passage through some designated space

Of beast, or man. You got used to the stench;
The mud was worse than being under fire,
My father said. A detail left the trench
At night, to get the dead back from the wire,

And no one volunteered. They stood, to view
Our brief exchange of rings and vows, for both
Our fathers had survived that war: and knew
Of death, and bright entanglement, and troth.

P. K. PAGE

After Rain

The snails have made a garden of green lace:
broderie anglaise from the cabbages,
Chantilly from the choux-fleurs, tiny veils —
I see already that I lift the blind
upon a woman's wardrobe of the mind.

Such female whimsy floats about me like
a kind of tulle, a flimsy mesh,
while feet in gumboots pace the rectangles —
garden abstracted, geometry awash —
an unknown theorem argued in green ink,
dropped in the bath.
Euclid in glorious chlorophyll, half drunk.

I none too sober slipping in the mud
where rigged with guys of rain
the clothes-reel gauche
as the rangy skeleton of some
gaunt delicate spidery mute
is pitched as if
listening;
while hung from one thin rib
a silver web —
its infant, skeletal, diminutive,
now sagged with sequins, pulled ellipsoid,
glistening.

I suffer shame in all these images.
The garden is primeval, Giovanni

in soggy denim squelches by my hub,
over his ruin
shakes a doleful head.
But he so beautiful and diademed,
his long Italian hands so wrung with rain
I find his ache exists beyond my rim
and almost weep to see a broken man
made subject to my whim.

O choir him, birds, and let him come to rest
within this beauty as one rests in love,
till pears upon the bough
encrusted with
small snails as pale as pearls
hang golden in
a heart that knows tears are a part of love.

And choir me too to keep my heart a size
larger than seeing, unseduced by each
bright glimpse of beauty striking like a bell,
so that the whole may toll,
its meaning shine
clear of the myriad images that still —
do what I will — encumber its pure line.

W. W. E. ROSS

The Diver

I would like to dive
Down
Into this still pool
Where the rocks at the bottom are safely deep,

Into the green
Of the water seen from within,
A strange light
Streaming past my eyes —

Things hostile;
You cannot stay here, they seem to say;
The rocks, slime-covered, the undulating
Fronds of weeds —

And drift slowly
Among the cooler zones;
Then, upward turning,
Break from the green glimmer

Into the light,
White and ordinary of the day,
And the mild air,
With the breeze and the comfortable shore.

DAVID WEVILL
Diamonds

Every man
Carries a scandal
At his heart.

The woodpile hides
A baby, or
A dead wife's bones.

In an ice-house down by the lake
On the damp sawdust, a coffin holds
The baker who went out hunting "to steady his nerves."

Nature a memory now —
Don't raise wild sap in a frivolous tree.
The land will not remember,
Or the sand, or the old stockbroker
Who drank his last martini in the lake one autumn night.

Leaves shake in the dust
Along the summer roads;
A cow gives birth to her calf, the world
Goes slack. Blood dries on the tines of straw.

And hay-stalks whistle through the field
Where a rusted car, its glass knocked out
Moans in the sun beside a plough,
A lesser ribcage, half-buried.

The pineforest
Heavy with dinosaurs —
In their depth the black is moving —

Blueberry bushes in the scrub
Stained our pails and fingers,
Boy, girl, and the breath of the blue juice.

And later the dirt,
Outhouse, hole of a mother skunk,
A prickle of flies and disease, streaming over the lake
To spider islands . . .

We killed a crow by the rainbarrel,
Peppered it with B-B shot.
Three nights the crow slept in my bed,
The fourth day I took and broke my gun.

Later I made amends —
My mind the temper of the lake
Changing like the color of an eye,
Or rooted: an Algonquin burial mound
Whose hair of cedar hides the old scalp wound.

In the slow fall of needles
Two old pines
Remembered they were man and wife.

Faded blueflower curtains,
Pinewood walls,
Pimples plucked by flashlight in the mirror —

This house was my body once,
My first two skins, water and wind.

Now shadflies go the way of salt
Over a shoulder, through the pores of screens.

Such delicacy as I caught
In the nighthawk's cry, the kindred
Whip-poor-will, like the cry of a young tree

In its growth . . .
The nail is in the tree's heart,
Hammered home with the flat of a shoe.

The house is up for auction soon.
Small fish turn tail and plunge through the pools of oil
To fresher waters.

I,
Down the same darkness,
Retrieve my lost diamond.

ANNE WILKINSON

Lens

I

The poet's daily chore
Is my long duty;
To keep and cherish my good lens
For love and war
And wasps about the lilies
And mutiny within.

My woman's eye is weak
And veiled with milk;
My working eye is muscled
With a curious tension,
Stretched and open
As the eyes of children;
Trusting in its vision
Even should it see
The holy holy spirit gambol
Counterheadwise,
Lithe and warm as any animal.

My woman's iris circles
A blind pupil;
The poet's eye is crystal,
Polished to accept the negative,
The contradictions in a proof
And the accidental
Candour of the shadows;

The shutter, oiled and smooth
Clicks on the grace of heroes
Or on some bestial act
When lit with radiance
The afterwords the actors speak
Give depths to violence,

Or if the bull is great
And the matador
And the sword
Itself the metaphor.

2

In my dark room the years
Lie in solution,
Develop film by film.
Slow at first and dim
Their shadows bite
On the fine white pulp of paper.

An early snap of fire
Licking the arms of air
I hold against the light, compare
The details with a prehistoric view
Of land and sea
And cradles of mud that rocked
The wet and sloth of infancy.

A stripe of tiger, curled
And sleeping on the ribs of reason
Prints as clear
As Eve and Adam, pearled
With sweat, staring at an apple core;

And death, in black and white
Or politic in green and Easter film,
Lands on steely points, a dancer
Disciplined to the foolscap stage,
The property of poets
Who command his robes, expose
His moving likeness on the page.

TWO

CURATORS' FORUM:
NOTES AND COMMENTARY ON THE SELECTIONS

Biographical Notes for Regional Curators
(in order of appearance)

Born in 1962 in Ghana, **Kwame Dawes** moved in 1971 to Jamaica, where he spent most of his childhood and early adult life. Author of eighteen books of poetry—most recently *Duppy Conqueror: New and Selected Poems* (Copper Canyon Press, 2013)—as well as books of fiction, nonfiction, criticism, and drama, he has edited nine anthologies and numerous collections by other poets. He is the Glenna Luschei Editor of *Prairie Schooner* at the University of Nebraska, where he is a Chancellor's Professor of English. He also teaches in the Pacific University MFA in Writing program, and he is a faculty member of Cave Canem, an organization committed to cultivating the artistic and professional growth of black poets in America. Dawes is the Director of the biennial Calabash International Literary Festival in Jamaica and Associate Poetry Editor for Peepal Tree Press. In 2012, Dawes established the African Poetry Book Fund and Series, which publishes four new books of poetry from Africa each year. Dawes's many awards include the Forward Poetry Prize, several Pushcart Prizes, The Shestack Prize, the Hollis Summers Poetry Prize, the Silver Musgrave Medal, an Emmy Award (for a documentary on HIV/AIDS in Jamaica), the Hurston/Wright Legacy Award, a Guggenheim Fellowship, a Barnes and Nobles Writers for Writers Award, and most recently the Paul Engle Prize, which celebrates a pioneering spirit whose contributions improve the world through the literary arts. Home website: http://www.kwamedawes.com/wp/.

Ishion Hutchinson was born in 1983 in Port Antonio, Jamaica. His poetry collection *Far District: Poems* (Peepal Tree Press, 2010) won the PEN/Joyce Osterweil Award. He has earned degrees from the University of the West Indies, New York University, and the University of Utah. Honors include a Whiting Writers' Award and the Larry Levis Prize of the Academy of American Poets. His work has appeared in *Ploughshares, Granta, The Huffington Post, Poetry Review, Caribbean Review of Books, Poetry International* and *The Los Angeles Review*, among other publications. He is the Meringoff Sesquicentennial Assistant Professor of English at Cornell

University and a contributing editor to the literary journal *Tongue: A Journal of Writing & Art* (tongueoftheworld.org). Home website: http://ishionhutchinson.com/.

Rustum Kozain was born in 1966 and schooled in Paarl, South Africa. His first collection of poems, *This Carting Life* (Kwela Books/Snailpress, 2005), won the Ingrid Jonker Poetry Prize and the Olive Schreiner Award. His second collection, *Groundwork* (Kwela Books/Snailpress, 2012), won the Herman Charles Bosman Award. He is the joint-winner of the Nelson Mandela Poetry Prize and winner of the Philip Stein Poetry Award and the Thomas Pringle Award, and he has received scholarships from the Andrew Mellon Foundation and the Fulbright Foundation. His poems, short stories, and reviews have been published in regional and international journals and his poetry has been translated into French, Dutch, Spanish, Italian, and Indonesian. He has edited poetry and fiction anthologies, has worked as a translator, and has taught literature, film, and creative writing. He is a manuscript reviewer for Kwela Books and lectures at international conferences and literary festivals. Home website: http://kozain.com/.

Les Murray was born in 1938 in New South Wales, Australia, and he grew up in Bunyah, about two hundred kilometers northeast of Sydney, on his widower father's dairy farm. Since 1965, when his first book of poems appeared, he has written more than forty books of poetry, prose, verse-novels, and essays; his most recent publications include *Killing the Black Dog: A Memoir of Depression* (Black Inc., 2009; Farrar, Straus and Giroux, 2011), *Taller When Prone* (Carcanet, 2010; Farrar, Straus and Giroux, 2012) and *New Selected Poems* (Carcanet, 2012). He has also edited numerous anthologies, including *The New Oxford Book of Australian Verse* (Oxford University Press, 1991) and many of the *Best Australian Poems* volumes (Black Inc.). He was the longtime editor of *Poetry Australia* and is currently literary editor of the journal *Quadrant*. Among other distinctions, Murray has been awarded the T. S. Eliot Prize, the Queen's Gold Medal for poetry, and the Australian Literature Society's Gold Medal. In 1989 he was made an officer of the Order of Australia for his services to Australian literature. He continues to live in his hometown of Bunyah.

Hinemoana Baker was born in 1968 in Christchurch and raised in Whakatane and Nelson, Aotearoa/New Zealand; she has lived for more than twenty years in Wellington and Kāpiti. She is a poet, recording artist, singer-songwriter, and broadcaster. Her first collection of poetry, *mātuhi | needle* (Victoria University Press, 2004), draws on aspects of her mixed Māori and Pākehā heritage. She descends from the Ngāi Tahu tribe in the South Island, and from Ngāti Raukawa, Ngāti Toa, and Te Āti Awa in the North Island; she has non-Māori heritage as well, with ancestors from England and Bavaria. Baker's second collection is *kōiwi kōiwi | bone bone* (Victoria University Press, 2010). She is co-editor of the anthology *Kaupapa: New Zealand Poets, World Issues* (The Development Resource Center, 2007). She has performed and read her poetry internationally and has released five CDs of music and poetry. In 2009 she was the Arts Queensland Poet in Residence; in 2010 she was one of thirty-eight writers in residence at the University of Iowa International Writing Program; and in 2012 she and eight other New Zealand poets and songwriters showcased their work in New York City. Along with her writing, singing, and producing, she works as an editor and teacher. Home website: www.hinemoana.co.nz/.

Sudeep Sen was born in New Delhi, India. He is the author of a dozen books, including *Postmarked India: New & Selected Poems* (HarperCollins, 1997), *Distracted Geographies* (Wings Press, 2003), *Rain* (Mapin / Gallerie, 2006), *Aria* (Mulfran Press, 2011), and *Blue Nude: Poems & Translations* (Partridge / Penguin Random House, 2014). He is the publisher and editorial director of Aark Arts and has edited several anthologies, most recently *The HarperCollins Book of English Poetry* (HarperCollins, 2012). He has directed the Delhi International Literary Festival and been a visiting scholar at Harvard University and a writing fellow at Sanskriti Foundation in New Delhi and Shanghai Writers Association in China. He won the 2007 Kathak Literary Award for his contributions to Bangladeshi literature, and the 2009 A K Ramanujan Prize for his translations of South Asian and world poetry. His poems have been translated into over twenty-five languages, and his writings have appeared in the *Times Literary Supplement, Newsweek, Guardian, Observer, Independent, Financial Times, London Magazine, Literary Review, Harvard Review, Telegraph, Hindu, Outlook,* and *India Today*. In

2013, he was the first Asian invited to deliver the Derek Walcott Lecture at the Nobel Laureate Week in Saint Lucia, and the same year he was awarded the Government of India Ministry of Culture's senior fellowship for "outstanding persons in the field of literature." Home website: http://www.sudeepsen.net/.

An Anglophone of Irish, Scottish, and English ancestry, **Todd Swift** was born in Montreal in 1966, and he holds British and Canadian citizenship. His blog Eyewear, with over a million hits, exemplifies his eclectic curiosity, with posts on James Bond, theology, Morrissey, and the blunders of the Tory party being as likely as not. Since 1988, when he co-edited the anthology *Map-Maker's Colours: New Poets of Northern Ireland*, he has been a prolific anthologist, producing many collections, including *Language Acts: Anglo-Quebec Poetry, 1976 to the 21st Century* (co-edited with Jason Camlot; Vehicule Press, 2007) and *Modern Canadian Poetry: An Anthology of Poems in English* (co-edited with Evan Jones; Carcanet, 2010). He is the author of eight volumes of poetry, including most recently *England Is Mine* (DC Books, 2011), *When All My Disappointments Came at Once* (Tightrope Books, 2012), and *The Ministry of Emergency Situations: Selected Poems 1983–2013* (forthcoming from Marick Press). His poems have appeared in many anthologies, including *Open Field: 30 Contemporary Canadian Poets* (Persea Books, 2005), *The New Canon: An Anthology of Canadian Poetry* (Véhicule, 2005), and in *The Best Canadian Poetry in English* (Tightrope Books, 2008 and 2012). From 2004 to 2012 he was Oxfam Great Britain's Poet in residence, and to raise funds he created three poetry CDs, a DVD, and a book of Young British Poets. He holds a PhD in Creative & Critical Writing from the University of East Anglia, and he has taught creative writing, critical theory, and English at universities in Hungary, England, and Scotland. In 2003 he moved from Paris to England and lives now in Maida Vale, London, where he is director of Eyewear Publishing Ltd., a small independent press focused primarily on poetry. He is a convert to Roman Catholicism from the Church of England and is married to Irish lawyer Sara Egan. Home website: http://toddswift.blogspot.com/.

Essential Poems from Ghana

by Kwame Dawes

There is nothing comprehensive about my list, which represents poems from Ghana that I admire and enjoy. I have tried to convey my joy in the comments that follow. Much of the work of Ghanaian poets is hard to find; however, this is, I think, a good start. I have focused on the more senior poets, as should be clear, as I fear that their work is slowly disappearing because of neglect. The good news is that there are quite a number of younger Ghanaian poets working today.

To complete this selection, I scoured my library of African poetry, Ghanaian authors, and quite old journals (some of which have ceased to exist). I also managed to secure a number of anthologies through libraries around the country, and drew on those to make my selections. Rather than attempt to create something of a canon, I simply sought to feature poems that appealed to me and that I thought would give new readers a fresh perspective on Ghanaian poetry. In many ways these poems are evidence of what I like to think of as the peculiar manifestation of modernity evident throughout African literature, which is characterized by a fruitful if not fraught interaction between Western modernist ideas and practice and traditional, largely oral practices and prosody.

[*Editor's note:* Due to permission constraints, we are unable to include two poems selected for this anthology: Kobena Eyi Acquah's "Variations Upon a Walcott Theme" and "Lamentations on an Oblation"]

∼

In **"In the Dungeon," Kwadwo Opoku-Agyemang** (born 1952) does not allow platitudes to consume his subject. The surprising informality and colloquialism of the poem's first line—"You guessed it"—unsettle the reader, as if what is to come will be light-hearted and easy, despite the fact that the poem is called "In the Dungeon." This poem is one of Opoku-Agyemang's often raw and relentlessly honest meditations on the West African side of the Middle Passage. Here is a Cape Coast man reflecting on his hometown as the launching pad of a major human atrocity, in as startling a line about the holocaust of slavery as you will find: "A slave is as naked / As a peeled vein / In a dream." But this poem's distinct contribution is its almost confessional lament for those who remained on the African side of the Atlantic—those who were not captured, if you will: "We buried dust inland / With anger and a voice / And a dozen brave words." Opoku-Agyemang's stark, resonant images capture rootlessness, exile, and the untethered sensation of the enslaved: "There are dogs, wet-eyed / Without owners." Is this what freedom should be? At the end of it all, the matter is not resolved.

Opoku-Agyemang is at his best in poems that employ the seemingly simple device of personification to create works of deep emotion and unresolved disquiet. **"Cape Coast Town"** pays homage to his hometown, employing sharply drawn and evocative images to contain both his pleasure and his unease with this home. I am drawn to the poem for the way it captures a sense of place and time that is neither sentimental nor dismissive: "the irrational streets"; "The night-mud houses" with "Their eyes half-shut"; and of course, the striking image of a town that has carried so much history inside it—"An aged town / It stands on the one good foot / Shaking and forgetful." Cape Coast is an important coastal town in Ghana; here Opoku-Agyemang reminds us that it is not a dead city but one in which blood still flows even as the speaker is witness to the ongoing and tragic hemorrhaging of a continent.

More than any other Ghanaian poet, **Kwesi Brew** (1928–2007) seemed to understand himself as something of a poet laureate, not so much out of vanity but out of a profound commitment to the project of writing poems that somehow captures a sense of the national project. Many of his most familiar poems are known for their public declarations, their seemingly unquestioning Christianity, and their propensity towards cliché and accessibility. Brew, however, was more than that, and the poems that delight me most in his oeuvre are those that are less assured, those that are playful, and those, like **"Adam and Eve and the New Paradise"**— with its final image of the "communion of crows"— that are daring in their political commentary. Here Brew recasts at least one part of the creation story, effectively declaring God dead or indifferent to the machinations of humans, and then recounts what is essentially an all-too-familiar narrative of African coups, corruption, and war. Paradise is, of course, lost, but the pragmatic actions of someone like Eve, whom he declares to be free of corruption and who is defined by her classic (for the West African woman) skill in business, would seem to suggest some hope. Unfortunately, Paradise remains abandoned: "The garden has run to weed," he writes, and "The garden homestead, now deserted, is used for synods . . . / By a communion of crows."

Easily one of the best-known and to my mind most accomplished of Ghana's poets is **Kofi Awoonor** (1935–2013), whose combination of ritual, proverb, political sensibility, and elegant modernist lyricism allowed him to produce a remarkable body of work rich with wit and sensuality. His confidence in his Ewe voice and culture made him more likely to reshape English prosody than for English prosody to alter him. Until very recently, he has never stopped holding a university post in or outside of Ghana, and he has been affectionately called "Prof" by Ghanaian friends and writers.

"My God of Songs Was Ill" explores the relationship between the poet and the idea of inspiration. For Awoonor, the muse does not arrive in the style of a Western European female figure, but in the form of what other West Africans might call the "chi"— a familiar guardian spirit that, while separate from the individual soul, is inextricably attached to the soul. The space between the inner self and the "god" in this poem allows for the kind of irony and wit that only a few African writers have managed to use without rancor or satirical agenda. The "god of songs" is restless and ill, and the poet seeks out some wisdom and guidance from the elders of his community. The bathetic advice that the elder offers first—"Come in with your backside"— is wonderfully funny even as it undermines any self-indulgence in the poet. Ultimately, the elder sends the artist to his father to find some meaning and healing, as well as some forgiveness for the violation. The singing god is a trickster of sorts, a troublemaker who suddenly heals himself and begins to sing only when things get dire. The final claim is Awoonor's articulation of the function of inspiration: "My god burst into songs, new strong songs / That I am still singing with him."

In the late 1970s, along with comrades and friends, Awoonor was jailed for political reasons at the Ussher Fort Prison in Ghana. During that period there was uncertainty about his future, and while in prison he witnessed the deaths of some of his companions. Awoonor's collection *The House by the Sea* is just one of a select body of poems written over the past fifty years by African writers in prison. Awoonor's poetic sequence, however, stands out for its understated wrestling with the meaning of life and death, and with ideas of home and exile. Among his most elegant poems, the sequence is complicated by a tension between hope and futility. Memory is important to the poet, as is the constant presence of death. **"Sea Time"** is a touching pledge to a friend facing a firing squad. There is nothing maudlin about this song; it is a meditation on the role of the living in remembering and learning from the patterns of the dying. The poem expresses defiance against death; the business of eating eggs and waiting for more eggs represents that hope. The poet does not embrace the martyrdom of a "crown of thorns" for his friend Kojo Tsikata, but something more glorious, a garland of roses for his friend's wounded knees. Awoonor faces the possibility of his friend's death by confronting the prospect of his own death, declaring that if necessary he will row his own ferry across to the other side. In *The House by the Sea*, Awoonor also reflects on the unreliability of those who should be in solidarity with him. These poems reveal the terrible effect of political imprisonment, not only on the body but on the psyche of the imprisoned. Although Awoonor could not have known this at the time when "Sea Time" was written, his friend Kojo Tsikata would survive the death sentence.

If there is a single poem that might well be described as a Ghanaian classic in English, it is Awoonor's graceful allegorical poem **"The Weaver Bird."** Its meaning is fairly easy to work out, of course: the weaver bird represents the colonial interlopers who come into Africa and effectively desecrate and take over the continent. (In his novel *A Grain of Wheat*, the Kenyan poet, critic, and political thinker Ngugi wa Thiong'o popularized what may have been an old Kikuyu saying: to paraphrase, "the white man came and told us to close our eyes and pray, and when we opened our eyes everything had been stolen.") In Awoonor's poem, the weaver bird is not demonized in simple or obvious ways. Indeed, the poem is less about the weaver bird than about those who stood by and watched, fascinated by the weaver bird: "We did not want to send it away." What began as a curiosity—a kind of Edenic fascination— ends with the transformation of the weaver bird into "the owner" and a preacher offering salvation. Beneath this delicate use of language seethes a sardonic anger that only appears in the final lines of the poem: "The old shrines defiled by the weaver's excrement." Tellingly, the weaver is no longer a bird but a conniving creature. Still, the "victims" of the weaver are not let off the hook. They allowed the weaver bird to stay, albeit innocently. At the end, the original owners of the home are left homeless, left with the challenge of finding their own rituals, their own language of worship, their own myths and sense of self. This is the classic post-colonial narrative, contained in a compact and clever poem.

~

Best known for her fiction and plays, which are shot through with remarkable poetry, **Ama Ata Aidoo** (born 1942) has helped shape Ghanaian and African writing. The theme of **"Totems"** is, of course, familiar: the loss of culture, the destruction of rituals (most likely due to colonialism and modernity). At the end of the poem, the speaker says she does not need to be reminded by her sisters to lament the loss of the legacies of the past. As with most poems of this nature—dirges, laments, and elegies—the very act of singing the lament represents a return to ritual and, to some extent, to hope. What stands out here, however, is the sense of loss and tragic mistrust brought on by marriages that are entered into—but fail— to "carve out destinies." The propensity for unfaithfulness in the male is aligned with the unfaithfulness of the colonizer. Those who speak platitudes about the security of roofs are clearly not trustworthy; even the man who seems most reliable is using his own family cloth to swaddle the illegitimate children he has fathered. Tellingly, Aidoo speaks to her sisters (both literal and figurative) whose shared wisdom and strength constitute hope in the face of betrayal. In this poem, Aidoo enacts one of the more powerful gestures of Ghanaian women, which is to challenge the traditional proverbs of the community and to create new proverbs that speak to the interest of women; these proverbs reveal that culture is never static but is constantly reshaped by imagination and experience.

~

Kojo Laing (born 1946) is best known as a novelist of somewhat experimental and entertaining fiction. His poem **"Godhorse,"** with its sudden leaps and elusive allusions, differs from much of what I have collected here. The premise of the poem—a grand allegory, it would seem—is puzzling. There is a horse; there is an old man who, as the rider, seems at times to grow young. And then there is the mysterious Mansa, the goddess of the breasts of incense. Fetish priests and bishops make appearances. The interplay between the horse, the rider, and Mansa is filled with sensuality, some violence, and not a little tension. Yet the landscape that the horse traverses (and eventually halts in) is the barren landscape of Ghana, which we first encounter with the scatological allusion to horse dung staining kente, the prized Ghanaian cloth, and then saluting the city of Accra. Laing creates tremendous energy and movement in the horse's journey. In the end, what is left is the persistence of beauty: the man, "poor, old . . . died with a smile before he hit the ground: / and under him were the crushed birds—O God, / carrying their expanding beauty still, still."

~

Atukwei Okai (born 1941) has often been regarded as a poet interested in engaging the rhythms of African drumming in his verse. Okai's poems avoid slavish devotion to a forced rhythm for its own sake. Instead, his poems manage to draw on the ritual language of praise, curse, worship, and lament even as he writes a spare and tightly managed line, rich in imagery and marked by a sardonic wit. In **"Watu Wazuri,"** the line "Rhododendrons in donkeydom" suggests that in a world of philistines and donkeys, the heroes listed here stand out as resilient flowers. Okai incorporates Swahili words in his poems ("Watu Wazuri" means beautiful people), and he feels comfortable invoking the music of Stevie Wonder and Ray Charles to evoke the legend of Kwame Nkrumah, Ghana's first president, and the tragic story of Miriam Makeba, who for much of her adult life had to live in exile from her home country of South Africa. Okai's eloquent lament for Nkrumah is created with a few deft strokes: "no sooner had you folded your mat / and gone beyond the corn-fields // than the victoria falls / the namib desert / and the table mountain // burst out in tears / and fire . . ." In a few words, Okai creates a complex narrative of euphemism and a reconstruction of history. Nkrumah is the one who walks away; he is not forced out—this is an optimistic and perhaps less than historically accurate accounting, but it is a kind of vanity, an articulation of myth-formation to which poetry often lends itself. There is dignity here. In performance, no doubt, the chants at the end would not seem as familiar as they do on the page.

~

Given the date (20 May 1994) noted at the end of **"Rwanda,"** it is probably a relief that **Ishmael Fiifi Annobil** (born 1958) chooses restraint and virtual silence to address the quite unspeakable horror of the genocide in Rwanda. He is unable to speak of blood and yet unable to contain the howl that ends the poem, a howl that belongs not to the speaker but to the darkness. (A howling darkness is an especially arresting image.) The discord of the moment affects everything; from the surreality and "wrongness" of toadstools in the noses of soldiers to the "off colour" of the rainbow, we are dealing with a world that is out of kilter. The dashes that mark the stop-start of ideas at the beginning of the poem create non sequiturs, stammerings that reflect the failure of language to manage this terrible news. Annobil manages to capture all of this in a very small space, a compact and cramped place that seems wholly inadequate to the size of the tragedy to which it speaks. The most striking and haunting image in this poem is, "The red glint of / Blades of an / Apocalypse." The machete was the weapon of choice for the killers.

~

In **"Caliban,"** **Abena Busia** (born 1953) invokes an old trope that all writers from places colonized by the British have to contend with in some way or another—the Shakespearean image of Caliban, Prospero's slave. Her reading of Caliban is "straight," at least at first. Essentially paraphrasing, she pares Caliban's fundamental argument down to its most basic parts: the mastering and mastery of language. The fact is that even in this small selection of poems by Ghanaian poets, we are engaged in the Caliban dilemma. Each of these poets has another tongue that is not English; many, like Kofi Anyidoho and Kofi Awoonor, write in this other tongue, but their reputation as poets is based on their mastery of English. Busia recognizes this as something of a trap, and in "Caliban," Busia departs from the Caliban mythos for a moment to explore the gender implications of this dynamic. Instead of finding her identity in Caliban, she locates it in the little girl who has been raped, victimized, which actually overshadows and, I might add, replaces the Caliban mythos, as a way to make metaphorical the African experience through the prism of gender. What is lost is innocence, and the echo of Blake ("little girl lost") is clearly intentional. Busia allows the poem to become autobiographical, thus making it serve as an introduction to her constant themes: the loss of her father; the blackness and African origin of her father; her sense of exile; the effort to make sense of her existence on "saxon shores." In "Caliban," Busia spells out what is lurking inside all the poetry included in this selection.

～

"Dying Birth" by **A. W. Kayper-Mensah** (born 1923) provides none of the usual railing against death and offers no spiritual assurance of an afterlife; there is just the power of the imagination to capture the sensation the speaker feels at the thought of death. Although the allusion to Saint Paul's declaration in the New Testament ("for to me, to live is Christ and to die is gain") is intended, Kayper-Mensah's sense of gain is not the reward of an afterlife but the reward of genuine rest and the imagination. This kind of coolness—almost pleasure—at the prospect of death can seem disturbing, and yet, in its simplicity and clarity, the poem convinces us that this sentiment is not only profoundly sane but also quite appealing. The most elegant stroke of the poem comes at the end, where the speaker contrasts the fantasy of an escape, a holiday from the world, to the chaos and lamentation that takes place at the news of the speaker's death. The entire fantasy smacks a bit of vanity, of course, but we are all familiar with this vanity, this hope that there will be lamentation at the news of our death. The speaker has only one concern—being able to prepare for the vacation.

～

Kofi Anyidoho (born 1947) is probably the best-known Ghanaian poet working today. His poems, like those of his fellow Ewe poet Kofi Awoonor, draw heavily on Ewe language and traditions even as they commit themselves to the larger project of writing a nation's identity through lyric and public poetry. In **"Doctrine & Ethics,"** Anyidoho makes use of a form of mythic folktale to construct a philosophical meditation on God and the place of God in our world. The poem, shot through with irony, is strikingly nonconfessional in its commentary. I am impressed with the way this poem, though filled with ideas about God, ultimately never quite states who God might actually be. That, no doubt, is Anyidoho's point:

perhaps God is unknowable, or—even more troubling, given the efforts of those the poet calls "they"—perhaps God does not exist. A key line of the poem—"And kicked God in the Face."—challenges this notion: in that instance, God becomes the victim of the children, and his capacity to be victim allows for the possibility of his existence. Without being heavy-handed, the poet manages to create virtual folktales about the ways various religions construct and use God. For Anyidoho, it seems God is a construct, and a fit subject for an elegy.

The Caribbean: Further Tropics

by Ishion Hutchinson with Andre Bagoo, Christian Campbell,
Kendel Hippolyte, Nicholas Laughlin, and Tiphanie Yanique

Joseph Brodsky has been quoted as saying "if Literature is the deity, the Anthology is our Bible," and though Brodsky's anthology has the pyramidal capital A, I doubt he is referring to one sole compendium ever published but rather to the varied personal reading experience every literature lover holds dear. The word bible, after all, just means book, and if Brodsky has anything as specific as the King James Version in mind, he is speaking in the valley of its plurality and of the limitless horizon such a book offers, which is the deity itself, Literature.

There are many anthologies, and every anthology is personal, and here with me five poets from the Caribbean collect and talk about their unauthorized anthology—thirty poems from eight nations and territories, which they believe to be among the strongest to come from the Caribbean region. I use the word *unauthorized* to make clear that the thirty poems about which our poets write are not to be perceived as an authoritative list of the best of Caribbean poetry. In fact, this small anthology is not interested in dangerous and ultimately meaningless superlatives like "best"— although certainly some poems that have been considered "classic" in the Caribbean oeuvre are present—but these poems are being introduced (or reintroduced) to you, reader, because they are the ones that light fires in our contributors' heads. It has been a great delight and blessing to read what Andre Bagoo, Christian Campbell, Kendel Hippolyte, Nicholas Laughlin, and Tiphanie Yanique have written in response to poems they love.

Our exchange came about partly because of our common geographic bond but chiefly due to the deep admiration I have for their work as poets and writers. For the most part we are similar in age, children of the post-independence island classrooms, where Caribbean literature was part of what stirred our love for words and our desire to become poets. Not surprisingly then, our own work directly and indirectly communicates with many of the poems you will read here. (In fact, you'll find poems by two of our contributors included in the selection, chosen by their peers.)

Personal admiration for their work aside, I am grateful these five poets have agreed to take part in this exchange because I believe they belong to a magical coterie of people laboring, in different ways, to ensure the active presence of Caribbean literature in the region and the world. **Nicholas Laughlin,** for instance, edits the *Caribbean Review of Books,* undoubtedly the best recent literary serial in the region; he is also codirector of Alice Yard, an experimental creative space in Port of Spain, Trinidad, as well as programme director for the Bocas Lit Fest, an annual literary festival based in Trinidad and Tobago. **Andre Bagoo** is a prolific journalist who also writes articles about Caribbean art for his popular blog. **Christian Campbell** is a cultural critic, a scholar, and a professor at the University of Toronto. **Kendel Hippolyte,** one of the Caribbean's leading dramatists, recently edited an anthology of poetry from Bermuda, *This Poem-Worthy Place;* he also cofounded the Lighthouse Theatre Company in Saint Lucia and is a key figure in the art and educational movement there. **Tiphanie Yanique** founded the Rock Collective, a poetry organization in Saint Thomas, and along with being coeditor of this whole anthology, she is a professor at The New School in New York City, where she teaches courses on Caribbean poetry and fiction.

I won't burden you with how hard we found working our way to these poems, under conditions no labor union would have tolerated. In the end, it was exhilarating to read through many poems and to write about them, but brutally sad to have to store so many away because we'd reached our quota of thirty for the entire region.

I can sincerely say that each of my cocontributors exemplifies what Eliot describes in "The Function of Criticism" as the quality of a true poet-critic, "who has so much to give that he can forget himself in his work . . . can afford to collaborate, to exchange, to contribute."

Hearing a poet speak about a poem can, sometimes, equal the pleasure of reading the poem itself and often becomes a kind of blessing. Discussing for the public something so intimate as a poem is difficult and delicate work, but after their long engagement with these poems, these five contributors magnify the poems they discuss without any proselytizing or academic shoptalk, even as they occasionally summon scholarly terms to clarify some poems' external contexts. Mainly those contexts involve the twin horns of geography and history, which curl back onto themselves as soon as they extend outside of the Antilles, so that a reader unfamiliar with the territory may miss some of the subtleties the poems contain. But of all the various contexts, of utmost importance to us as readers is language, the very material of poetry.

The strange terms are delectable. They give immediate sonic pleasure. But what else is expected of them, and how do you receive what lies beyond the new sounds these poems put into your mouth? Not just the words' etymological life, but their tastes and textures? How to ratify the subplot of their native cosmos? What romance or violence is here?

In such instances, there is great fortune in having responses from poets who are capable of taking you far past the surface of local sounds, poets who can "show riches" as Caliban did to Stephanos and Trinculo, lost on the strange island. No one is better able to induct you into the mythical sphere of these poems than my companion poet-editors. Their comments are never as gratuitous as a guidebook's know-it-all, nor merely honorific reveries on Caribbean verse yet to be widely appreciated; instead, they offer thoughtful distillations that can help a reader—especially the reader new to Caribbean poetry—see through the "spear of night" (as in Aimé Césaire) into the "light and the people on whom the light falls" (as in Derek Walcott).

The wish, always, is to have the poem without a middleman, to read it on its own terms (or listen—which you can do when audio files and video clips can be found online. I trust, reader, that you won't disappear at the end of these introductory comments but will feel invited to a greater banquet, one you will attend on your own, reading and re-reading the larger body of work written by the poets presented here. You may feel compelled to do so as a matter of personal investigation, to measure against your own responses what we've said about the poems we've chosen. This is encouraged and expected. You will quickly discover enormous worlds beyond the cues we have given. You will wander into lively pantheons of image and phrase, music and play, sensation and instinct: the tropic no tourist-board advertisement has the fire to capture.

It is no exaggeration to say that this bountiful exchange between poet and poem has become a kind of choral work, something more than mere dialogue. A poem sings a call and the poet hums an answer, and a circle takes shape, as in an early childhood game where every person gets the chance to be the lead singer whom other people chorus around. The leaves are clapping in your hands. When you are exiled to a desert island, make sure these poems are sewn into your clothing's hem, or in case you can't have all thirty hidden that way, fold at least a handful into the pages of books that the miserly ruler allows you to take along.

—*Ishion Hutchinson*

~

THE BAHAMAS

"In the Marketplace" by **Marion Bethel** (born 1953) offers a nuanced meditation on the Caribbean diaspora by exploring the migration of an upper-middle-class Bahamian girl to Toronto to attend boarding school. Bethel frames the poem with a twisted nursery rhyme: "to market to market / to buy a new tongue / home away home away / brigidum brum." Bethel expands and messes with the idea of the marketplace as a site of exchange where anything can be bought and sold: fruit, vegetables, fish, tongues, hips. Above all, it is the voice—playful, tender and knowing—in the poem that keeps me coming back: "my father coloured / colonial and Christian / existed somewhere / between somethingness / a putative son of the enlightenment / and the namesake / of Marcus Garvey." The speaker doesn't romanticize diaspora, which is a painful process of loss, transforming language and desire: "I discovered the new market / had no pumpkin cassava peas corn / breadfruit dilly okra grits / this market had no grunts / and goggle-eye fish / and I had no stomach / for trout bass, sweet pears." Give thanks for these lines (which are tattooed somewhere on my skull): "the part of me / I share / with you / was not bought / in the marketplace."

—*Christian Campbell*

~

"Iguana" by **Christian Campbell** (born 1979) begins, simply enough, like an occasional poem: "My friend from Guyana / was asked in Philadelphia / if she was from 'Iguana.'" What follows is a bravura linguistic and lyrical exercise, soaked in rage. The voice of the poem employs a kind of newsreel technique, rattling off facts about words that resemble the word "iguana." In the process, the voice suggests the richness and complexity of the region with grace: "The earth is on the back / of an ageless iguana. // We are all from the Land of Iguana, / *Hewanorra*, Carib name for Saint Lucia." But the poem is not only a protest, it is also a kind of elegy, ending memorably with two lines that complicate its meanings: "And all the iguanas scurry away from me. / And all the iguanas are dying."

—*Andre Bagoo*

⌒

BARBADOS

"Stone" (excerpted here) is the **Kamau Brathwaite** (born 1930) poem that stays with me more than any other in his overall necessary oeuvre. The first line, the poem's refrain, haunts: "When the stone fall that morning out of the johncrow sky . . . " This poem is a eulogy for the late, great dub poet Mikey Smith, who was stoned to death in Jamaica in 1983 at the age of twenty-nine. The poem both dramatizes Smith's death and séances his voice from the dead in his inimitable cut-throat wail: "lawwwwwwwwwwwwwwwwwwwwwwwwwwwwwwwwwwwwwwd."

"Stone" has the percussive intelligence we find in any Brathwaite poem and in any Mikey Smith dub: "when the stone fall that morning out of the johncrow sky / I could not hold it brack or black it back or block it off or limp / away or roll it from me into memory or light or rock it steady into night." What is it with this poem? I want to say "velocity." I want to say "kinetic force." Then I realize that the poem itself is the stone hurtling across history: "I am the stone that kills me." This line, this poem, leaves me wrecked.

—*Christian Campbell*

~

GUYANA

I have seen analyses of **"Proem"** by **Martin Carter** (1927–1997) and I accept that analysis of poems may be a worthwhile pursuit, but confronted with a poem like this, another part of me wants to say that all that's really necessary is to intone it over and over, like saying a rosary. This is the Carter that causes some political firebrands (by no means all!) to shake their heads ruefully. But it is the enigmatic circularity of the poem—its actual rhythm a beautiful mimesis of the act of constant self-replenishment—that makes it an inexhaustible homage to poetry. I would be worried if the Caribbean poetic tradition did not contain poems like this one.

—*Kendel Hippolyte*

~

"Demerara Sugar" by **Fred D'Aguiar** (born 1960) creates its own vernacular in the way only the most memorable poems can, creating a powerful column of rhythms, meanings, sounds. Consider: "Sugar cut by hand-swinging cutlass / With half an eye kept on any snake / Wrapping its way around cane fields // Cane pressed for its last ounce of sap / Boiled down to molasses that is cane . . ."

D'Aguiar does not describe but suggests the great physical effort required to manufacture sugar, and evokes the psychological hardships endured by slaves and later by the indentured laborers who were brought to the region to work to make things sweet for others. In "Demerara Sugar," there is no punctuation; there is no full stop; sentences appear suspended but also flow into each other like prose: this is a sea of words that forms its own narrative across lives and across times.

—*Andre Bagoo*

⌒

The poem **"The Carpenter's Complaint"** by **Edward Baugh** (born 1936) is a Caribbean descendant of the tradition of complaint poetry reaching back to Chaucer. A dramatic monologue in Jamaican patois, it triumphs and delights in local gestures without becoming a pastiche of the familiar scene it captures. It is twenty-five lines of theatre, from the sharp *in medias res* opening to the exclamatory end—"it burn me, it burn me for true!"—in which we encounter through one occasionally vituperative voice a universe that is peopled not just with those respectable old-fashioned Caribbean names mentioned but also with an actual community, listening and talking, whom we witness. Because of the monologue convention, we don't hear them speak but have the pleasure of imagining their voices, which provides the carpenter the necessary shelter to reminisce in his time of crisis.

—*Ishion Hutchinson*

⌒

One of the striking qualities I admire in the poem **"Yap"** by **Kwame Dawes** (born 1962) is the way the natural world appears to conspire and converge on Yap (a derogatory term for homosexual); the bigots are not just the school bullies but the sinister environment of "crows circling" and "walls scarred with obscenities." The poem does not assume anything about Yap's inner turmoil, though we can guess at this, easily; rather, the reader confronts with Yap the hard facts of the place he cannot escape.

—*Ishion Hutchinson*

⌒

The brilliant, incantatory poem **"To Us, All Flowers Are Roses"** by **Lorna Goodison** (born 1947) commands multiple registers of

Caribbean speech. It begins with etymology: "Accompong is Ashanti, root, Nyamekopon. / Appropriate name, Accompong, meaning / warrior or lone one . . ." This poem teaches me something important about form: it is catalogue, chant, map, rosary, a roll call of the hybrid (African, European, and more) Jamaican landscape. It is not a forced, uncritical celebration of multiculturalism, but a celebration of, and lament for, the land, and a singing of names: "There is Alps and Lapland and Berlin. / Armagh, Carrick Fergus, Malvern / Rhine and Calabar, Askenish / where freed slaves went to claim / what was left of the Africa within . . ." Goodison says simply, "There is everywhere here." This is delight birthed from terror.

—*Christian Campbell*

"What the Oracle Said" by **Shara McCallum** (born 1972) is about the endless search for meaning, for history, and for our own personal narratives. While knowledge is possible, it appears subjective and ultimately elusive: "The sky above you will shift in meaning / each time you think you understand." In addition to echoing the tone of the Pentateuch, the poem's form and rhythm mirror the drift of surf on a gently sloping seashore, building to its last lines: "But nothing will be enough. / The sea will never take you back." This is a poem haunted by the poet's past.

—*Andre Bagoo*

A dirge whose dream-like images evoke longing for a lost place, lost time, lost affection, **Shara McCallum's "What the Oracle Said"** closes a sequence of mermaid poems in her first book, *The Water Between Us* (1999). For the mermaid, the price of love—or what looks like love—is the loss of her home, the sea. Like the taint of original sin, the scar of separation lingers: "The shadow of your scales / will always remain. You will be marked / by sulphur and salt." There is no solace in this damaged world where "stone will be your path." This is a song of exile from family, homeland, the hopes of the past.

—*Nicholas Laughlin*

~

"If We Must Die" by **Claude McKay** (1890–1948) is perhaps the most famous Caribbean poem—and yes, it is a Caribbean poem; after all, Claude McKay, though some seem to forget, was a Jamaican-American poet. Yes, Winston Churchill recited it, and countless others, and still it is also mine. "If We Must Die" is our great rallying cry, our anthem of resistance: "If we must die, let it not be like hogs / Hunted and penned in an inglorious spot." What I find so fascinating about McKay's great poem, radical in its resistance to anti-black, anti-colonial violence, is that it is a sonnet. The poem builds a formal and political tension between the speaker's resonating cry for freedom and the sonnet form's constraints, so a phrase such as "pressed to the wall" becomes meta-discursive: "Like men we'll face the murderous, cowardly pack, / Pressed to the wall, dying, but fighting back!" This is the engine of the poem; the raised arms of McKay's exclamation marks up against the decorum of his iambic pentameter. His constant pushing against that European form, also his to claim, embodies the sense of fear/lessness, captivity, and resistance of his time and of all times.

—*Christian Campbell*

~

Anthony McNeill (1941–1996) is an angel I wrestle with, knowing that someday he will bless me. His poetry-faith is so unflinching that on entering his later work you sometimes feel you are intruding on deepest privacy. His earlier work is more accommodating and I've always loved **"Hello Ungod,"** a poem that I find students instantly connect with. There is so much post-apocalyptic scenario, inner and outer, condensed into this grim un-prayer. I remember a delayed shock at "the easy prescriptions / have drilled final holes in my cells," which refers to radiation sickness such as the survivors of Hiroshima and Nagasaki still suffer. And the macabre image of "head sieves in the wind" reaches me with its resonances of the futility of intellect in the presence of human-made destruction on such a massive scale. That ambiguous last line is masterful. The cruel irony of using a litany as the structuring form of the poem is brilliant; McNeill weaves into his litany the motif of telecommunication, that defining feature of the twentieth century, bringing an acutely modernist slant to the theme of spiritual despair.

—*Kendel Hippolyte*

~

In Vahni Capildeo's "Light and Dark," (also included here) light is a weapon, but in **"Some Definitions for Light (I),"** by **Kei Miller** (born 1978), light is life itself. "It is a poem about a poem," Miller recently said of this piece. The bulk of it consists of a series of definitions, including definitions for photo, photometer, photophobia, photogenic, and photographer ("one who writes about it"). In-between this newsreel style are characters and anecdotes. Miller brilliantly concludes by suggesting that a page with a poem is itself an illusion composed of "brilliant brilliant light"—and, thus, is also dark.

—*Andre Bagoo*

~

"Epitaph" by **Dennis Scott** (1939-1991) is one of the most haunting poems I have ever read on the fraught issue of slavery. It has a sense for me of a hard-won, precarious equanimity, of being barely restrained from tipping over into an unstoppable destroying rage, and yet the tough wisdom in the poem feels equal to the demands made on it—just barely. The poem's psychological stance is the one I feel most affinity with and would pass on as counsel to another generation. There is no flinching here from anything—not from the horror of the hanging, nor from the insidiousness of a tempting but nonetheless culpable amnesia on the part of the descendants of slaves. And along with all this, there is a perspective that the persona struggles to keep: an awareness of a wider life that must be maintained, even improved, though not at the cost of forgetfulness. Generations later, community continues, held together partly by shared story, even though at that point of the story there must always be a pause.

The poem's technical features are quintessential Scott. His handling of lineation, starting with that deft yet grave enjambment from the first to the second line and then similarly from second to third, is always exquisitely judged. And the apostrophe image—"like a black apostrophe to pain"—is so startlingly exact, the recognition is a wince. It must be rare for the image of a punctuation mark to work so hard and so well to create meaning. This is a poem that by the force of its gravity (and dense brevity adds to this impact) attracts the term "iconic."

—*Kendel Hippolyte*

~

The collections *Gardening in the Tropics* and *Over the Roofs of the World* by **Olive Senior** (born 1941) have been rightly praised, but in my view the ambition of her fourth collection, *Shell,* has not been properly appreciated. This work, like the other collections, is ostensibly a sustained meditation on a single theme. But Senior, who is a slippery and beguiling poet, takes one idea and mines all of its possibilities until it no longer appears to be what it was before. **"Peppercorn"** is, for me, the perfect distillation of what Senior does in the entire book, which is to say: she presents an elaborate conceit dealing with family and the history of the trans-Atlantic slave trade. The idea of the peppercorn—which evokes memories of the ancient native populations that grew it in the Americas—is metaphor for and mirror to the process of slavery: "we are jumbled, shaken up, / rolled together, little knowing our fate / or destination, till black and shriveled / by the sun, looking all alike now, we are / tumbled into hold of a ship for forty days / and forty nights (we guess — for black / is the fenestration)." History, again, is shown to be the elephant in the room, with modern ideas of sexual objectification being traced back to it: "if you'd only / allow me to do a striptease, slow, peel off / my black skin, you'd be pleased — / or shocked — to discover: I'm white below."

—*Andre Bagoo*

~

The title of **"A West Indian Poem"** by **Tanya Shirley** (born 1976) is a warning. The negative stance of the first lines aims to suggest a departure from the expected ideas for both the literature of the region and the region itself: "It is not the first time our house / has killed a bird . . ." The violence of the political process in Caribbean democracies—and in this poem, specifically the Jamaican democracy—is palpable on the surface: red is a key image representing blood (menstrual and otherwise) as well as the electoral ink used in the "impending election" to which the poem refers. A sense of dread and menace pervades the poem: "I thought of the woman rising from her evening prayers / shot dead in her house last night . . ." Echoes of the Old Testament abound, as does a sort of wry fatalism: "a dead bird's dried blood will remind them of God / and we shall be passed over." The Old Testament God has been replaced with new gods; the praying woman replaced by "dream stealers." The

Passover is now passed over. This inversion suggests the absence of salvation and hope.

—*Andre Bagoo*

~

MONTSERRAT

The phrase **"Behind God Back"** in the poem of the same name by **Howard Fergus** (born 1937) is a common one in the Caribbean for identifying faraway places, places that are backwaters and backward. It marks not only a place that is physically far away, but also a place far away in the general imagination. In this regard the Caribbean region itself might be "behind God back." In Fergus's poem the "two-be-three island / hard like rock" of Montserrat is behind God back. Long Ground, in the rural countryside of the island, is *really* behind God back. Being non-white is, in a way, being from behind God back, as we see that even the "People in the town . . . off-white and brown" are "rejected like stained cotton" when they arrive in England. Fergus keeps addressing the idea of the faraway place as a place where nothing is supposed to happen and no greatness is accomplished. His refrain undermines that: "They . . . never told you" the ways in which your Long Ground home was so important, vital, not only to you ("your mother strong") but even to England, to British commerce and intellectual history.

—*Tiphanie Yanique*

~

SAINT LUCIA

If Derek Walcott subtly gives voice to suppressed history within everyday life in his poem "Mass Man," then **Kendel Hippolyte** (born 1952) tackles history straight on. The opening line of the titular poem from Hippolyte's *Night Vision* makes this engagement clear: "It's hard to see anything without history." Yet, for Hippolyte the engagement with history—which is a central theme of much Caribbean poetry—is complex. The poem examines this complexity, at first acknowledging history as a key force that must be reckoned with, but then raising questions over what we find, and the usefulness of opening such a Pandora's box. "Because we see with history, / it is difficult to see through it," the speaker remarks in the opening section. "And yet we must / or we become it, become nothing else but history." By the poem's end the aspects of self-reflection and the cruel truths of history have wrought another kind of imperative: "The window blind will draw down like an eyelid closing, leaving / your self in the illumination that discovers you / only in darkness." In "History," another poem in Hippolyte's *Night Vision*, the speaker remarks: "Knowing that at the end / Death will acknowledge no identities / I can only half believe / in heroes, villains, histories."

—*Andre Bagoo*

∿

The music evoked in **"Saint Joseph at the Music School"** by **Jane King** (born 1952) might well be the music of the poem itself, but also the music of the sea, expressed in alliterative opening lines that economically create a powerful impression of the languid scene: "The wind susurrating the shak-shak trees / almost drowning the sounds of the sea / and the children performing for teachers / in the building behind me." The restless aura created here mirrors the attitude of the children at school as well as of the speaker, who is possibly a migrant, likely an outsider. But outside from what? Perhaps the voice is in mourning for a family, for a son: "Yesterday / we heard the archbishop say / Saint Joseph is the patron of a happy death." Thus the drowning sound of the sea, which is music too.

—Andre Bagoo

∼

"The Schooner *Flight*" by **Derek Walcott** (born 1930) is long and breathtakingly readable. Walcott depicts his struggle with history and identity and language through a tumultuous sea voyage taken by Shabine, a mixed-race sailor in search of an inner paradise that the outer paradise of the Caribbean promises but fails to give. Whether one agrees or not with Walcott's vision of the Caribbean's potential as a gloriously hybrid civilization, the language of the poem is a triumph of that vision. Throughout the poem, the energy is ferociously exuberant, fiercely true to actual speech that nonetheless modulates convincingly into sentences you would never hear in actual speech: "They kept marching into the mountains, and / their noise ceased as foam sinks into sand." The poem is full of language junctures like this, where the oral and the written traditions of literature meld, and both are extended.

"The Schooner *Flight*" is an enormously humorous poem as well, in places, and this humor makes up part of the persona's rough-edged, quick-witted self-protection: "I was so broke all I needed was shades and a cup / or four shades and four cups in four-cup Port of Spain." This is so outrageous, it ought not to work. But caught up in Shabine's hurricane energy, what to do? The language climbs to refined heights as naturally as it brawls, and at the end of the poem, it settles into a mode of benediction: ". . . And the light over me / is a road in white moonlight taking me home. / Shabine sang to you from the depths of the sea."

—Kendel Hippolyte

~

SAINT VINCENT AND THE GRENADINES

In Caribbean poetry, **Shake Keane** (1927–1997) is sui generis. To the best of my knowledge, he has no precursors and no real successors, though one may sometimes come across a poem or a spoken-word piece that reminds one of him. **"Per Capita Per Annum"** is a high-octane example of his style and vision, which are inextricably intertwined. I love the manic but always controlled energy. It's like Allen Ginsberg's "Howl," but the fury and sorrow are modulated by an irony that's too wise to break into a wail. Or like Aimé Césaire's, with a radical, anarchic flippancy. And the voice is so unmistakably Caribbean, inflected by the hyperbolic Midnight Robber style, the zany imagination of freewheeling street talk, so-called high-register and low-register vocabulary intermingling so as to render these distinctions almost meaningless. The critique of capitalism is harsh, merciless, panoramic. It is only Shake Keane's distinctively quirky delight in language that lightens, in every sense, one of the most mordantly dark poems to come out of the modern Caribbean.

—*Kendel Hippolyte*

~

TRINIDAD AND TOBAGO

The great subject of Lagahoo Poems, from which **"Wind, Water, Fire, Men"** is taken, is death itself. Using the guise of Trinidad folklore figures, in particular the Lagahoo—a shape-shifting spirit— **James Christopher Aboud** (born 1956) examines writing, religion, and the tension between spirituality and sex. But "Wind, Water, Fire, Men" goes beyond all of this and raises questions about the meaning and form of the soul. "Lagahoo takes his shape from the wind; / Wind has no shape," the poem argues. By the end of the poem, through a process of transmogrification, "Lagahoo came to touch his nature / And know its shape." What has happened in between is the manipulation of a series of hieroglyphic images that call into question the writing process, the possibilities of knowledge, and human ties to the natural environment.

—*Andre Bagoo*

James Christopher Aboud's Lagahoo poems can feel like fragments of a creation myth. His Lagahoo—a werewolf-like figure from Trinidadian folklore—is an alter ego, an ancestor, a sentinel, an unseen threat waiting for the fall of night. He defies gravity and time. He is nature itself, patient and hungry. And for Aboud, the reader senses, the Lagahoo also embodies an assertion of possession: he belongs to his island, Trinidad, as his island belongs to him. That belonging, he writes elsewhere in the sequence, is a "deep dark mud-lust and rebellion."

—*Nicholas Laughlin*

This featured section of the long sequence **"Land to Light On"** by **Dionne Brand** (born 1953) is an example of Brand's genius for animating syntax—syntax being what Paul Valéry calls "a faculty of the soul." In Brand's hands, the soul is vivid, continuously in flux, restless. The opening four lines, beautifully staccato, glimmer like far images coming into view. From there, as the images close in, the syntax folds into a serpentine whole—the "exact flooding" of pine, sea, road, hummingbird, desert blooms, and snows, and "grit in the mouth" that, as the speaker says, "is peace."

—*Ishion Hutchinson*

~

"Light and Dark" by **Vahni Capildeo** (born 1973) is a dazzling puzzle. The poem appears to present three voices and three distinct viewpoints, each of which ponders the possibilities of what it would be like to live on a planet with no light. The first speaker argues that "light, in its slightest manifestation, / will be worshipped — will it now?" A second speaker disagrees, saying: "Total and absolute is the love / of darkness. Light achieves / no more than clarity . . ." But a third voice then reveals: "as a matter of fact, on that planet / the sun is taboo." And therefore the first speaker is punished: "Brilliance on brilliance destroyed her / as, laid out like a starfish, / she smiled from her vanishing eyepoints."

This is a deeply political poem, alluding to the vagaries of power: how it is arbitrary, how the victors tend to oppress, how surface change often masks deeper truths, how truth itself can be manipulated. The first speaker poses a mere question, not an assertion. Her fate therefore appears arbitrary and oppressive. The third speaker's status is questionable: is this an omniscient narrator? To what extent can an omniscient narrator exist? Further, the assertion that light is "taboo" is ambiguous. Life on this planet where light is valued seems cruel, not bright. Thus one position, which asserts itself over another, is revealed to have no true moral center, as can happen in the political world in which each party of a two-party electoral system is as bad as the other. "Light and Dark" is a glimpse of the remarkable achievements of Capildeo's distinctive style, so evident later in the Trinidadian's other books *Undraining Sea* and *Dark and Unaccustomed Words*.

—*Andre Bagoo*

Vahni Capildeo is perhaps the most ambitious, certainly the strangest Caribbean poet of her generation. She is a restless explorer of form, a connoisseur of lexicon and linguistic register. A parable in

the form of a dialogue, **"Light and Dark"** muses on the limits of knowledge and imagination. Can we love what we cannot name?
—*Nicholas Laughllin*

~

"They Came in Ships" by **Mahadai Das** (1954–2003) takes on the Caribbean "grand narrative" of *kala pani*, Hindi for "black water," describing the journey of indentured laborers from India to the Caribbean. The brilliance of this poem lies in both its intimate and distant visions of our history. Das begins in the sweeping way we expect of this kind of historical poem: "They came in ships / From far across the seas / Britain colonising the East in India / Transporting her chains from Chota Nagpur and the Ganges Plain. / Westwards came the *Whitby* / Like the *Hesperus* / Alike the island-bound *Fatel Rozack*." But then she steers the reader elsewhere with these startling images: "They came in fleets of ships. / They came in droves / Like cattle. / Brown like cattle, / Eyes limpid, like cattle." She confronts the *kala pani* head-on, but her poly-vocal approach resists monolith and rejects simplistic nostalgia of origins. And then she gifts us with a cryptic beauty: "I, alone today, am alive." This is our great *kala pani* poem.
—*Christian Campbell*

~

"Ode to My Unknown Great-Great Grandmother" by **Lelawattee Manoo-Rahming** (born 1960) reads: "I heard you were the first / to belong nowhere. / Born on the wide Kala Pani / between Calcutta and Port-of-Spain / on a ship unknown." It complicates a simplistic nostalgia for origins with an incredible intimacy, framing the speaker's barrenness against the ancestor born on the un-mappable sea.
—*Christian Campbell*

~

Crepuscular, modest, and epigrammatic, **"Peelin Orange"** by **Mervyn Morris** (born 1937) is like the rings in a pond, spreading far and wide. The gesture is always casual, "Dem use to seh" is the mark of a true rumor-monger but how quickly and skillfully the poem descends from the impersonal "Dem" and "yu" into the personal "mi" and "mi father" in the second stanza. Yet even there the impressions remain stark—did the father "teach" by holding the boy's hand or did he instruct from a distance, verbally? One might think that there is something cold here; yes, but it is a warm coldness. Note the subtle humor throughout, brilliantly underscored by the line breaks and the ironic emphasis gained in the single-word lines: "perfec," "break," and "peelin." The reticence here is well mastered and I love the nonplussed philosophical ending; I smile but know I should cry.

—*Ishion Hutchinson*

~

We must give thanks for **"Discourse on the Logic of Language,"** a strange and brilliant poem from the magnum opus, *She Tries Her Tongue, Her Silence Softly Breaks* by **M. NourbeSe Philip** (born 1947). With Brathwaite, Philip is among the most important practitioners of a Caribbean innovative poetics. Philip fractures language and makes it stutter: reverb or echolalia? To read this poem, the page must be spun like a turntable. Something must move; someone must move. To read this poem, you need a crew. But the truth is, because of Philip's marvelous disrespect for boundaries of genre and form, it's often not clear where a poem begins and ends in *She Tries Her Tongue*. Is "Discourse on the Logic of Language" a combination of many poems or one poem? Is it a series of Lyotardian language games? Is it an act of theory? How do you read a poem in which one part runs vertically down the margin on the left side of the page while another runs more conventionally down the middle and another floats horizontally near the middle of the right side? Philip continues to ask and ask again: "Where is my mother tongue?" and "What is a poem?"

—*Christian Campbell*

~

In **"Haiti," Jennifer Rahim** (born 1963) takes the difficulties of understanding a new language and applies them to the problem of understanding the world (and Haiti) itself. History is not the only subject of this subtle poem, but also cynicism: "A secret has passed between you / so wonderfully terrible, // it laid your cities prostrate." Rahim suggests that the difficulties of recognizing and acknowledging local forms of language mirror our inability to come to terms with the problems not just of Haiti, but also of our lives: "For the earth has spoken, / to you, her magma Creole." Observe the craft, such as the pun in the second stanza: "Full-throated syllables, up- / rising from deep down." The poem is at once about Haiti and not about Haiti.

—*Andre Bagoo*

~

THE VIRGIN ISLANDS

Although **"'Pon Top Bluebeard Castle Hill"** by **Habib Tiwoni** is about an adolescence now gone, it defies the usual coming-of-age version of this narrative trope. The youths here make their way through a lushness of land. Like teenagers everywhere, they play their games ("I was king") and have their intimacies ("scratches /

on a lover's back") but these are also children who really know this land beyond just a stomping ground. They know the names of the birds and of all the flowers; they know the taste of the basil and feel of the casha; they know the difference between the genders of a papaya; and they know how to free the honey from the bees. So when we read the line "the senses awoke one day" we can't quite believe it—the senses of these youths have been particularly awake and aware. But it turns out that the youths have missed something. The land that is theirs in their love and knowledge is not theirs at all. This poem, while seemingly about adolescence, is also about the Virgin Islanders of all ages who once could walk the islands and pick fruit and sip honey freely, but now find themselves faced with various blockades (fees to pass through, gated committees, condos literally blocking the way) that suddenly make them trespassers on their own land.

—*Tiphanie Yanique*

As with Tiwoni's poem, **"Noontide, Fort Christian"** by **Marvin Williams** is focused on a particular space in the landscape of the Virgin Islands. Examined here is an old Danish fort that sits on an island harbor. The fort is now painted "ripe-wound red" which, despite the suggested violence of the color, is more intriguing for tourists than the original dull grayish white. The poem suggests that the harbor, usually presented as a place of great beauty, actually has an ugliness all over it—the sun is not the welcoming sun of the tourist brochure, it is a "niggering" sun. The boats in the harbor are not picturesque, but are "huddled, besieged." The tourists, with their maps and cameras, do not see—or perhaps refuse to see—the full complexity of their surroundings: The fort was originally used to hold slaves.

—*Tiphanie Yanique*

Twentieth-Century Poems from South Africa
by Rustum Kozain

It is necessary when writing about almost anything in South Africa to explain the use of racial terminology, even if, and especially when, one does not endorse the use of such terms. The country's colonial and apartheid history produced stark divisions, in public and private life, based on labyrinthine notions of race; the racial terminology has been used as shorthand to provide broad social and political contexts. The apartheid terms for the major "race" groups were black (African), "coloured" (mixed-race), Indian (descendants of indentured laborers and immigrants from the Indian subcontinent), and white. People of Chinese descent were classified as "coloured." These terms are still used in official, formal, and informal contexts: officially to inform state policies of affirmative action; formally, as in academic discussion; and, informally, in casual conversation. These terms still inform most South Africans' primary view of themselves and each other.

Because of the influence of Steve Biko's Black Consciousness ideas in the 1970s (inspired partly by the Black Power movement in the United States), there is also a tendency to use "black" as an umbrella term for African, "coloured," and Indian. While there were and are significant economic and cultural differences among these three groups, the use of an inclusive "black" served as a political assertion and, in discussion, as shorthand. It will be clear from context in my commentary that follows whether I am using "black" either inclusively or in distinction from "coloured" and Indian. While use of the word *coloured* (sans quotation marks) has become more acceptable, I mark my protest at this term with scare quotes.

The poems from South Africa featured here are listed chronologically with regards to their first publication in book form.

[*Editor's note:* Due to permission constraints, we are unable to include two poems selected for this anthology: Gcina Mhlophe's "Say No" and Mongane Wally Serote's "City Johannesburg."]

～

The later poems of **Arthur Nortje** (1942–1970), including his **"Native's Letter"** of 1970, arrived on the cusp between the "silent decade" of the 1960s and the renewed vigor in South African cultural life as a younger generation came of age—chiefly, of course, Steve Biko—and renewed the resistance to apartheid. But "Native's Letter" is also a poem from afar, written in Toronto, Canada, and one that tries to come to terms with the relationship between the émigré writer and the home country left behind. As in most of Nortje's poems, there is a shimmering carapace over the text, something that some critics may read as an excess of style. The tone, though, is one of estrangement, the tone par excellence of the exile, which by necessity ruptures the surface of the lyric. This has parallels with much of Joseph Brodsky's poetry, characterized by a deep resignation, the estranged self somehow caught and reflected in the apparently casual opening line. The speaker of the poem—the lyric subject—is not present to him or herself.

"Native's Letter" twists through varying styles: elevated vocabulary ("apocryphal," "supremacy," "amnesia"), tropes from Romantic poetry (weeping at a shore, melancholy), and idiomatic expression ("tough as nails"). Here Nortje works to establish his voice as he comes to terms with the conditions of exile and explores the way the exile may keep alive the memory of alternative, suppressed South African historical figures (Tshaka, Hendrik Witbooi, Adam Kok). The poem also nods at a cosmic sense of history that may provide hope against the overwhelming force of apartheid. Moreover, the poem asserts that somehow exiles may work through various media to bring the South African situation to public attention.

Poetry is one such medium and the poem ends on a note that sug-
gests Nortje is a poet struggling with an exilic guilt as well as with
the guilt of someone engaged in an activity as ineffectual, politically
speaking, as poetry. What comes from a position of (self-)doubt is
in this way resolved: "for some of us must storm the castles / some
define the happening."

Nortje's poetry is, to a large extent, a tortured contest between
expressly political themes (local and global) and broader existen-
tial issues of the alienation of the self. There is an autobiographical
foundation to this, as well: Nortje was classified as "coloured" in
apartheid South Africa and his (unknown) father was Jewish. In a
country obsessed with rigid racial classification, it is not surprising
that his engagement with the racial politics of South Africa of the
time should find expression in his poetry.

~

The short poem **"In Detention"** by **Chris Van Wyk** (born 1957) uses
a simple trick to brilliant, powerful effect, showing up the absurdity
of the official reasons often given by the apartheid state to explain
the deaths of many anti-apartheid activists while in police custody.
The poem starts in the plain, matter-of-fact language of reportage
taken from actual official explanations: "He fell from the ninth
floor / He hanged himself / He slipped on a piece of soap while
washing." These lines are repeated in different order, but then the
poet starts to switch words around, until we get:

> He slipped from the ninth floor while washing
> He fell from a piece of soap while slipping
> He hung from the ninth floor
> He washed from the ninth floor while slipping
> He hung from a piece of soap while washing

The repetition of officially given reasons already exposes the absurdity of the apartheid state's predictable and bloodlessly mantra-like responses. By amplifying that absurdity, the poem produces macabre comedy and adds a tone of urgency. Whether the apartheid state cared about its credibility at the time or not, the poem represents these "reasons" as a desperate scramble by the authorities to be believed. The poem remains a classic of the times.

~

In **"The Plumstead Elegies,"** a long poem (more than twenty pages in length) that echoes Rainer Maria Rilke's "Duino Elegies," **Peter Horn** (born 1934) addresses a range of issues in South Africa, including the role of and need for political expression in art, especially in the context of a highly repressive society. Some lines excoriating the dismissal of political art in favor of aesthetic value reach a pitch of lyrical intensity difficult to gainsay. The poem is from Horn's third volume, *Silence in Jail* (1979), which was banned for a dozen years after its publication.

~

Using language as theme both literally and figuratively, **Jeremy Cronin** (born 1949) in **"[To learn how to speak . . .]"** expresses the broad anti-apartheid vision of the late 1970s into the 1980s. Culturally, the historical—and persistent—racial divisions of South Africa are reflected in linguistic division: black South Africans are typically proficient in at least one African mother tongue and either English or Afrikaans (and many black South Africans will speak more than one African language plus English and/or Afrikaans), while the overwhelming majority of "coloured," white, and Indian South Africans (myself included) often speak only English and/or Afrikaans. Needless to say, such linguistic division was both a tool and a result of apartheid educational policies. Here, the poem's literal anti-apartheid theme—"To learn how to speak / With the voices of the land"—is much more than a riddle, moving effortlessly among different registers of a linguistic South Africanness: suffixes for Afrikaans place names; a moon poeticized into an African image (a "cow-skinned vowel"); African-language vocabulary taken up in both English and Afrikaans; working-class slang; and English influenced by African-language inflected pronunciation (as in, for example, "the 5.15 ikwata bust fife / Chwannisberg train," which refers to the 5:15 or quarter-past-five Johannesburg train). He also incorporates from Afrikaans the words *stompie*, which means "little stump," or "little butt," usually a nickname for a short person; *golovan*, meaning a small cart, possibly from *cocopan*, which is a South African noun for a mine cart; *songololo*, or "pill millipede," from *Nguni ukusonga*, meaning to roll up.

As if aware of its utopian impulse and the near impossibility of its task—South Africa, after all, remains wracked by its apartheid-based socioeconomic and cultural divisions—the poem remains protean and multivalent, a quality marked by its syntactical trickery. All its main clauses lack a finite verb, instead making use of infinitives: "To learn," "To parse," "To trace," "To write a poem," "To voice without swallowing," etc. These parallels are part of the poem's lyricism. By using the infinitives, the poem inhabits an ambiguity between yearning and action, yet avoids the sermonizing didacticism that its theme could easily have given into.

Set in prison, **Jeremy Cronin's** long poem **"Walking on air"** tells the story of an ordinary white working-class man caught up in political activity and thus incarcerated. He is presented with a hard ethical choice, makes the correct one, and so ends up "walking on air." Part of the attraction of this poem is how skillfully Cronin brings dialogue into the poem.

~

Andries Walter Oliphant (born 1958) in **"Childhood in Heidelberg"** recalls the childhood experience of apartheid-forced removals. Its tone is gentle and unassuming, and its details are imaginative and mysterious, filling in a childhood of "fun" until the child's awareness changes.

~

Probably South Africa's foremost poet, **Kelwyn Sole** (born 1951) is known for his complex political poetry. A long love poem with a night of sex as its central topic, **"Conjunction"** is direct, explicit, and fresh in its images.

~

"Our Sharpeville" by **Ingrid de Kok** (born 1951) is another poem recalling childhood during apartheid, but this poem is spoken from the viewpoint of a white girl. In tone similar to Oliphant's "Childhood in Heidelberg"—even, gentle, unassuming—"Our Sharpeville" weaves together a complex experience: a grandmother cautions the girlchild not to watch passing black men by sexualizing the encounter: "They do things to little girls."

In the pressure cooker that South African society had become by the 1980s, suffering itself was graded in perverse ways. **Ingrid de Kok's "Small Passing"** responds to one such example, exploring the idea that a white woman's suffering of a miscarriage is of no consequence compared to the kind of suffering poor black women experience. "Small Passing" seeks to establish a solidarity among women by describing black women reaching out with support and empathy to the white woman.

～

In **"Blessing," Kelwyn Sole** adopts the voice of a teenage black girl, Blessing, who witnesses the murder of an unknown man by "third force" vigilantes. (People now commonly accept that in the late 1980s and early 1990s, the South African security establishment was sponsoring such proxy forces.) This is a remarkable persona poem in which Sole, in a country with obstinate social divisions, inhabits the identity of someone at such a vast social and educational remove from his own. The poem is also important as it "puts paid" to certain arguments of authenticity, arguments that were big debates in cultural and literary circles at that time.

～

"Dark Rider" by **Tatamkhulu Afrika** (1920–2002) is a rare pastoral poem from a poet who was known for his descriptions of marginal characters' lives, mainly in his home city of Cape Town. In gentle tones, this poem describes a visit to a landmark location on the slopes of Table Mountain and within walking distance of the city center. The ominous note of "the desolate breath of the void" then leads to an intriguing structural anomaly in the next stanza, already hinted at by "there" used as adverb and pronoun for the place. While the poem describes a visit to, and the speaker's activity in, the pastoral location, it is unclear where the speaker himself is located. To emphasize this dislocation, a spectral "dark rider" passes by, perhaps as an image from boyhood adventure tales: cloaked, with a sparkling buckle and "the white moth of a hand," the figure's face is "forever not seen." In the end, the speaker admits that this may be all dream (as in many ways any pastoral poem always is). But here the central fascination remains that the dream *in* and *of* the pastoral involves a dislocation in locution, and that even in dream a colonial figure appears as "sentinel."

~

Jeremy Cronin's prose poem **"Running Towards Us"** bears witness to a gruesome event: a man, seemingly beaten and stabbed to death, is doused with gasoline and a tire is rolled closer in preparation for his "necklacing"—that is, the tire will be placed over the body, thus locking down the arms, and the body will then be set alight. This kind of violence was part also of the internecine violence that plagued poor communities during the late 1980s and early 1990s, often caused by "third force" elements (state-sponsored vigilantes known as *witdoeke*, or white bandanna) and "comrades" (young men aligned with the African National Congress). As the speaker and his companion decide to turn around and leave the area, cautious of getting caught up in the simmering mob, the "corpse" gets up and starts running. The poem ends by bringing the wounded, running man as a nightmare figure into the present and future of South Africa and its negotiated settlement. The poet is prescient, as the morbid symptoms symbolized by the running man are ever-present, more insistently so, in today's South Africa.

~

Kelwyn Sole's "Housing Targets" is, like Cronin's "Running towards us," a critique of the present government and its haphazard, lacka-daisical, and half-hearted attempts at social reconstruction, recalling a past where "we believed in a future." The poem's imagery appears as fantasy, revolving around negatives and empty spaces, captur-ing at once the fragility and desperation of the country's poor as they wait for government largesse to trickle down into meaningful contribution.

Favorite Australian Poets

by Les Murray

A great many Australian poems are favourites of mine. This is a selection from the riches. Eleven of them were first published in the twentieth century, while those of Ashlley Morgan - Shae, Robert Gray, Margaret Harvey, and Tom Coverdale are very recent. Similarly, most of the poets are or were Australian-born, while three have been domiciled in Australia. One of these is New Zealander Jennifer Compton, long resident in New South Wales, and Alan Gould is of English and Icelandic parentage. Another, Billy Marshall Stoneking, eventually returned to the USA and reclaimed his American citizenship (he now lives in Australia again), but his poem is a unique case. As a young immigrant teacher from West Virginia in the 1960s and early 1970s, Billy Marshall, as he was then known, worked in schools in remote inland Australia. There he became friends with initiated Aboriginal elders who passed along elements of their belief and custom to him—their sacred lore, as we might say, though they would call it their Law, and mean no pun by that. In the manner of another white poet, Roland Robinson, a generation earlier, Billy Marshall took what had been told to him in a mixture of indigenous language and contact-English and transported it into a more dignified form, in line with Western literary practice. In the traditional Aboriginal world, all poetry is sung; what Marshall worked from was "Outside" accounts, so called, intended for an uninitiated man, in this case a friendly foreigner. His versions came out in the early 1980s in a fine book titled *Singing the Snake,* but much that underlay that book didn't belong to the Western calendar at all. Interestingly, in the same period and in the desert region, the renaissance of Aboriginal non-figurative painting, which has since gone around the world, was just getting started. Much of that painting, of course, is done, as it were, in code, to protect sacred content. We on the outside delight in the intricacy, the sumptuous colors, the haunting gesture and design, yet nothing is really given away. Our critique is baffled and kept at an essential remove. Taking that hint, and from much gloomy experience, I have become gun-shy of ever seeing poetry on the same pages as critical commentary . . . For this reason, I offer no more apparatus with this mini-anthology. Not even potted biographies: those can be got from the internet, if wanted. Now enjoy the reading, and feel free to cough.

Fifteen Essential Poems from Aotearoa/ New Zealand

by Hinemoana Baker

It's difficult to choose only fifteen poems to represent the nation. After doing a few somersaults and uttering a loud cry of distress, I decided to take a "six months on Mars" approach, asking myself "Which fifteen poems would I take with me to Mars? Which fifteen poems would give me continuing rewards upon re-reading? Which New Zealand poems could I not live without?" So this is an unashamedly personal selection, which I hope at the same time makes a gesture at the scope of poetry written in the country today and in the relatively recent past.

It's safe to say that New Zealand is more progressive in its dealings with our indigenous people than many other countries. That said, there is still a relatively small number of Māori authors being published, and fewer of us are choosing a writer's life than I or many of my colleagues would like.

Most of us who are published are writing in English. By the 1980s, the Māori language had declined to the point of near-extinction because of the ongoing legislative and political effects of colonization. From the 1980s, it has enjoyed a kind of renaissance, thanks to the unfailing efforts of many activists over the decades. In some areas, parents can now send their children to Māori-language educational institutions from pre-school to university. We have a dedicated Māori-language television channel, now—an offshoot of another channel broadcasting in both English and Māori. And Māori is now one of three official languages in Aotearoa / New Zealand (along with English and New Zealand Sign Language). Even so, Māori is in a delicate position in terms of its long-term survival. Estimates of those who speak the language vary between 4 and 9 percent of the entire population.

Māori song-poems and chanted forms, which include mōteatea, haka, karakia, and waiata, are (and always have been) a vibrant part of Māori life in Aotearoa. They are the only word-based compositions that could be said to be truly and uniquely indigenous to this country. Māori composers and orators are held in high regard, and the creations of the most skilled ones are remembered, recited, and sung for many generations.

It is true, however, that Aotearoa is a nation of many cultures and languages now, and writers like Tse Ming Mok, Lynda Chanwai Earle, Aleksandra Lane, Kapka Kasabova and Teresia Teaiwa among many others give the lie to the idea that we are simply a bicultural nation of European settlers and indigenous Māori.

I feel the need, before turning to the poems themselves, to touch on a phenomenon we sometimes call "Tall Poppy Syndrome" here: instead of embracing and celebrating those of us who achieve on a grand scale, we sometimes prefer to ignore them, or cut them down. I'm sure this is not just a New Zealand trait, and of course this is a broad generalization. And more and more we are challenging this where we see it occurring. But there remain a few stand-out examples. One of our top-selling novelists offshore is Patricia Grace, and although she is much loved here, she is not as well-known in New Zealand as her success overseas would indicate. My own view is that one of the most important cultural gifts America and Australia can (and do) give us is a good strong lesson in confidence and self-belief, and in supporting our nation's high achievers.

Arts funding in New Zealand has suffered in the past several years of a National government (our version of the GOP, though I once heard someone say that the entire spectrum of New Zealand politics would probably fit within the U.S. Democratic Party). While our national arts funding body, Creative New Zealand, continues to offer residencies and grants to writers with a track record, and there are quite a few other sponsorships and stipends run by other government departments and private funders, it would be fair to say that sports do better than the arts in every budget, and compared to Europe and the United States, we have less of a tradition of philanthropy in support of artists. However, I am grateful to be living in a country where it is highly unlikely that I will be imprisoned or killed for what I write. I was in Pittsburgh briefly in 2010, as one of thirty-eight resident writers from around the world visiting the U.S. under the auspices of the University of Iowa's International Writing Program. While in Pittsburgh, I was fortunate enough to read and perform for an organization called "City of Asylum Pittsburgh," which provides residencies for writers in exile from their own countries. I met several extraordinary authors from Myanmar, China, and El Salvador who each told stories of imprisonment and/or torture. It was humbling and frightening, and made me very glad to have the freedoms that I do.

My selection is presented in reverse alphabetical order, which places Hone Tuwhare first and which fits perfectly with our Māori custom of honoring the elders (particularly those who have passed away). And in a way this order references the upside-downness of being here in the Antipodes.

~

"No Ordinary Sun" by Hone Tuwhare (1922–2008) reads like an elegy to the earth and to humankind. Tuwhare, our first Māori poet laureate, was also the first Māori writer published in English. "No Ordinary Sun" was one of the first poems I ever read—we studied it at school—and it has haunted me ever since. A very political character, Tuwhare had strong feelings about French nuclear testing in the Pacific, among many other things. "No Ordinary Sun" has been called an emblem of the peace movement.

I think it's safe to say that all of our major poets have written and published powerful elegies, whether it's Janet Frame's "Yet

Another Poem About a Dying Child" (also included here) or Dennis Glover's fantastically onomatopoeic "The Magpies," which is a kind of elegy to the rural economy set in Depression-era New Zealand. But for me, our most affecting elegies are the *waiata tangi*, the song-poem laments, created in pre- and post-European times by Māori composers, often also important *rangatira* (leaders) in their communities. Many of these were composed by women. Interested readers could investigate the series "Ngā Mōteatea," a collection of these *waiata* hailing mainly from the North Island's east coast tribes, and also a book called *Kāti au i konei,* a collection of these compositions from two of my own tribes, Ngāti Toa Rangatira and Ngāti Raukawa.

~

In **"Waka 99," Robert Sullivan** (born 1967) foregrounds Māori ancestor stories, our stories of creation and "discovery," without simply venerating them; rather, Sullivan re-envisions them, bringing traditional Māori stories and concepts alive in different ways. He references tradition, for sure, but he goes beyond reiteration to imagine a future when Māori treasures (canoes, for example) smash their way out of their various resting places—even out of the land itself—in a kind of ecstatic apocalypse, a "resurrection." "Waka 99" alludes to Māori accounts of how the North and South Islands of Aotearoa came to be. While there are several different versions of these stories, differing from tribe to tribe, the following is a brief and fairly popular version. One of our most revered ancestral *atua* (god) figures is Māui, who, with the help of his brothers, from a canoe called Nukutaimemeha, fished up the North Island, known as "Te Ika a Māui" (The Fish of Māui). Afterwards, it is said, the canoe with Māui's brothers on board became the South Island (Te Wai Pounamu to some, Ārai te Uru to others) and the Southern Alps mountains. Sullivan's poem also speaks of the discovery of our islands by the great Polynesian adventurer Kupe, in around 950 CE.

Most of all, what keeps me coming back to this poem is that chant about the veins: "blood relations / of the crews whose veins / touch the veins who touched the veins / of those who touched the veins / who touched the veins . . ." This is the best poetic translation of the word *whakapapa* (translated mostly as "genealogy," but so much richer than that single word) that I've ever seen or read. We revere our ancestors, and anything they are said to have touched is *tapu*, sacred, unbelievably precious to us, be it a weapon, a cloak, or a mountain. *Whakapapa* is at the heart of almost everything that Māori culture holds dear, and to see it given this kind of attention in a poem never fails to move me.

~

In **"The Stolen," Marty Smith** (born 1956) recounts recent and historical stories with political overtones yet avoids diatribe, rhetoric, and didacticism. "The Stolen" refers to a man called Te Kooti Rikirangi Te Turuki, a Māori leader, warrior, and prophet in the 1860s; the poem also speaks to a more recent event in which a painting by Colin McCahon, one of New Zealand's most celebrated artists, was stolen from the premises of the Department of Conservation in the Urewera National Park. Members of Ngāi Tūhoe, the local tribe, stole the painting in 1997 as a symbolic act designed to bring attention to the many acres of land taken from them and other injustices perpetrated by the colonial government. Weaving history with her own memories and a primordial visual reading of the landscape that would make McCahon himself proud, Smith has made a well-known political event—and a story that's frequently told— dramatic in the best possible sense of the word.

~

"On Our Knees or Homage to the Potato" by **Reihana Robinson** (born 1951) is a kind of prayer with political and historical implications. During the 1860s and 1870s, many Māori families and villages found themselves starving, their crops having been burnt to the ground by government forces greedy for land. In some ways, I cannot imagine a more violent act, both against the land and against the people, against their sense of themselves and their hope for the future. I also hear echoes of what was done to the Irish by the English in this poem. The colonizing impetus was in full force by the time it reached Aotearoa / New Zealand.

"Hotel Emergencies" by **Bill Manhire** (born 1946) conveys, through its incantatory language, the sense that the poem is being dictated by a higher power. Manhire, New Zealand's first poet laureate, has been a huge supporter for many of our local writers through his teaching. The real story of how that poem came about couldn't be less lofty: staying in a hotel in Denmark, Manhire noticed a sign in English that said "The fire alarm sound: is given as a howling sound. Do not use the lifts." Nevertheless, the poem speaks in a voice full of wisdom and sadness, a voice that might belong to someone very old, thousands of years old, an ancestor even, warning humankind of its own inevitable failings. Despite this, it ends on a hopeful note. Some have said it's too hopeful, perhaps a little sentimental. But for me, the word "smoke"—so pungent and quotidian—brings the poem back from that brink.

In **"I was a feminist in the eighties," Anne Kennedy** (born 1959) satirizes its own form at the same time that it makes a powerful point about the impossibility of living up to feminism's expectations. (In terms of feminism's influence or presence in New Zealand poetry, I would point interested readers towards work by Sia Fiegel, Tusiata Avia—who is included here—Cathie Koa Dunsford, Robyn Hyde, Janet Charman, and Teresia Teaiwa, for starters.) I come back to this poem again and again for its wit, and its insights, and its killer last lines.

~

"When I had a son in my early teens" is by New Zealand Jewish writer **Lynn Jenner** (born 1954), who won one of our most prestigious literary prizes with her first book, *Dear Sweet Harry,* which pushes the boundaries of genre and form. The Harry of the book's title is three different people, perhaps most notably Harry Houdini. The poem included here is not one of the Harry poems. It references one of the ways in which Jewish families tried to save their sons from the Tsar's army, and is one of several in the book that personalizes large-scale historical events such as World War I and immigrant experiences. Jenner's recent poetry, as yet unpublished in book form and part of her PhD work, explores loss, erasure, invisibility, and silence, which are all important themes in New Zealand literature for many reasons. The havoc and damage inflicted by these losses, for many generations, are comparable to those wreaked by what we think of as "war" or "genocide." And the ways in which people survive and even flourish after such losses seems to have a lot to do with how widely and loudly their stories are able to be told. From this perspective, Lynn Jenner is the kind of storyteller whose work I admire very much.

~

It's said that New Zealand literature often has a dark element, a kind of Antipodean Gothic. In fact this is something that's said about other art forms here, too; I've heard it most often about our films. The poem **"duck"** by **Bernadette Hall** (born 1945) has a real sense of locomotion, fueled by humor, grief, and despair; "duck" is one of the most moving poems I've ever read about the panic of grief, the lunatic ways we act when we are trying to avoid pain. And how one seemingly smaller, less significant grief can trawl up many others and break the heart open again.

~

In **"Yet Another Poem About a Dying Child," Janet Frame** (1924–2004) does nothing to romanticize or sanitize death or the afterlife, and makes no efforts to comfort anyone. The poem is honest enough to acknowledge that in these moments of paralyzing grief, such as that experienced when a child dies, there is no comfort. There is only pain, and sometimes rest from pain. I believe Janet Frame understood that: she led an extraordinarily rich literary and personal life, but was also subjected to some horrific injustices which saw her living in and out of psychiatric institutions for about eight years. Her three-part autobiography was made into the award-winning movie *An Angel at My Table.*

~

"How to live by the sea" by **Lynn Davidson** (born 1959) portrays the Kāpiti Coast, where I live. New Zealand is often seen by those overseas as an unspoiled paradise. This poem avoids the grand sweep of an aerial shot of snowcapped mountains in favor of a close-up, almost domestic focus. The ocean, the terns, and the orca all feel very much part of the life and considerations of the poet, as if there were no separation. There is something so intimate, almost wrong, about the image of the heron haunting the letterbox—ghostly beak and feathers instead of entirely unexceptional bills and postcards. I admire the warnings and disorder in this poem.

~

"Silly" by **Meg Campbell** (1937–2007) captures—despite its title—an undercurrent of repressed violence and frustration, illustrating the way life (for example, the dogs) gets in the way of our spontaneity, and chaos can ensue. Campbell was married to another beloved New Zealand poet, Alistair Te Ariki Campbell. She struggled with mental illness all her life, and she has written about her illness and about time spent in psychiatric institutions.

~

Kate Camp (born 1972) has a singular style, a ferocious intellect, and a bawdy sense of humour. **"Snow White's Coffin,"** the title piece from her most recent book, has a gravitational pull, with its fairytale echoes and the sense that this is a poem in mourning which at the same time is questioning what it means to remember, to care, to grieve. There is a story being told, certainly. And there are beautiful, sad flourishes: "they died like oceans / full of slow turbulence/ as if brought by death to life." To me, the poem is an elegy to a long-gone childhood, and also a raging against letting go of that Snow White dream. It is a howl, a shout, such as that which goes up in a crowd when a circus performer falls from a tightrope or a trapeze. It's a kind of ode to mortality.

~

James Brown (born 1966) has said that his poem **"No Rest"** owes some of its overstatement and ranting tone to one called "From a Recluse to a Roving I Will Go" from the book *A Hundred of Happiness and Other Poems* by British poet Martin Stannard. This could have been a much shorter poem, but I believe it would have lost a good deal of its humor and impact without its sheer size.

~

The work of **Jenny Bornholdt** (born 1960) shares a lot in terms of tone, I think, with the poems of Sharon Olds: acute powers of observation and exquisite pacing. I am delighted to include **"Wedding Song,"** because New Zealand has just passed Marriage Equality legislation, and I read this poem differently now, in light of that; somehow it feels even more jubilant and uplifting than before. It's not all roses, though—just like a real marriage. There's a "weta you find on the path, / injured by alteration." The *wētā* is an endemic insect here, much like a very large grasshopper or katydid, treasured for being indigenous yet also the stuff of many nightmares and phobias among those not fond of such creatures. So spouses should be prepared for tragedies, and for frights that turn to grief and for which there is no easy blame target. "The Author" supposedly no longer exists, so don't expect that language between you will be utterly reliable. And don't get irritable when you don't get the mail (reactions, messages, opinions) you were expecting. At least the post is getting through.

~

"Wild Dogs Under My Skirt" articulates **Tusiata Avia's** experience of being a New Zealand-born (in 1966), *afakasi* (mixed-race) Sāmoan woman, growing up in New Zealand in 1970s and 1980s. The title poem of her first collection, this is a radical claiming of identity, which is seen in the poem as completely immersed in *fa'a Sāmoa* (the ways of Sāmoa) and at the same time outside of that, aware of the pain it can cause. There's trust and there's wariness. The *tufuga* (master tattoo maker) is at once a threat to, and at the service of, the poem's protagonist. At the same time as she knows the *tufuga* "means me pain," there's a strong impulse to experience that pain, to have legs like "black octopus" that "catch rats and eat them," a reference to the traditional Sāmoan story of the rat that tricked the octopus into letting him ride on his head before defecating there.

Modern English Poetry by Indians

by Sudeep Sen

The history of contemporary English poetry by Indians is well over sixty years old—it has been almost sixty-five years since India became a Republic in 1950. To celebrate that political milestone, the poets included in this selection are all born post-1950 and all use English, which is just one of India's many official languages.

The editors of this anthology specifically suggested that I choose only Indian poets writing in English who are not United States nationals, so as to "bring to the U.S. the words of poets and poetics they might not have fully heard about just yet." Because of this particular constraint, other poets I might have wished to include had to be left out. I encourage further reading of anthologies and individual volumes by poets not represented here.

In this selection some established poets share the pages with relatively new, promising writers in a room without walls where individual and collective echoes are equally eloquent and important. My purpose as a practicing poet, translator, and literary editor is to offer a judicious selection of contemporary poetry written by Indians in English, one that presents an unusual and original wordscape of the vast multilingual, historical, and artistic terrain of India and the Indian diaspora. The selected poets live in India and in Europe, Africa, Asia, Australia, and the Pacific.

Although Indian poetry in English has, according to literary critic and novelist Pankaj Mishra, "a longer and more distinguished tradition than Indian fiction in English," surprisingly little is known about this literature. There are too few discerning anthologies of contemporary Indian poetry published in India, and even fewer abroad. That lack is a major surprise considering the vast cultural power of the world's largest democracy and India's position as the third-largest English-language publisher in the world.

I hope this selection of fifteen poems by the eight poets presented here helps to shift, remap, and expand the existing topography and tenor of contemporary English poetry by Indians. I urge readers to be open-minded, to read these poems in the historical and cultural context they are set in, and to read with an awareness that the Indian tradition goes back thousands of years and represents one of the earliest of the world's civilizations.

The range of style, preoccupation, and technique among these eight poets is expansive and impressive. This diversity and multicultural representation creates an internal dialogue between the poets and the varied topographical cultural spaces they come from or are influenced by. The poems create an inherent syntactical and historical tension—one that ultimately celebrates the written word.

Taking into consideration the quality of the contents in this mini-selection, I would provocatively assert that the best English poetry written by Indians in the contemporary national and international literary arena is perhaps as good or superior to Indian fiction in English as a whole. I believe that finally only the printed word matters, so I've provided no elaborate critical jargon, contextualization, footnotes, or explanations. All the poems selected here were included in *The HarperCollins Book of English Poetry* (HarperCollins, 2012), which I edited.

Born in 1962, **Amit Chaudhuri** (**"The Writers"** and **"Insomniac"**) is what I call "a poet's novelist." He is also a trained Indian classical singer who leads the Amit Chaudhuri Band, with albums such as *This Is Not Fusion*. A combination of creative writing and music is reflected in his poetry, which layers commentary, wit, reflection, reference to language and voice both heard and unheard, pun, image, and story with a sonorous quality of inflected music.

⌒

In **"Postmortem"** and **"Milk is Good for You"** by **Amitava Kumar** (born 1963) we see elements of this poet's talent as a prose writer and a documentary filmmaker. The prose poem is a difficult form to get right, especially the balance between what might be called short or flash fiction and a traditional prose poem. These two poems use elements of fiction with a particular poetic flair.

⌒

In **"Epigrams for Life After Forty"** and **"How Some Hindus Find Their Personal Gods,"** **Arundhathi Subramaniam** (born 1967) brings alive the quotidian with wit and wry humor in a language that is lucid and unpretentious. An understated feminism underpins much of her poetry. Subtle turns of phrase and immediacy in her verse draw the unsuspecting readers into her intimate word-world.

⌒

Michelle Cahill infuses aspects of mythology with modernity without losing the sense of urgency and passion that marks her sophisticated verse, as seen here in **"The Piano Lesson"** and **"Kālī from Abroad."**

⌒

Identity formation takes the form of staccato rap, and repetition provides a lyric structure and visual symmetry in **"Identity Crisis"** by **Priscilla Uppal**. **"Books Do Hold Me at Night,"** her poetic tribute to bibliophiles, asks how one can escape a love for books, the writer's dream and poet's best friend.

⌒

"Everyday Things in My Life" by poet and novelist **Priya Sarukkai Chabria** (born 1955) shows how a poet can stretch language and genre into innovative structures and form. The footnotes are part of the main body text of this long poem, as is the grid-spreadsheet motif. Contradictions animate this experimental poem: illusion and reality, truth and untruth, fact and fiction, utterance and silence.

~

The experimental poems **"Counsel"** and **"Invocation"** by **Sandeep Parmar** (born 1979) use language and verse structure in ways that are daring and boldly avant-garde. The bibliophilic details, couched literary comments, and the prose poem's paean to blood and the act of poetry makes her verse unusual and original in approach.

~

Vikram Seth (born 1952) is a poet of great formal play. **"Sampati,"** allegedly the world's shortest sonnet, contains only thirteen words and alludes to both Indian and Western mythology: Sampati and Icarus are juxtaposed and overlapping. **"For Philippe Honoré"** is a clever acrostic poem set in the sonnet form that poignantly details friendship, love, and the collaboration of the arts, in this case poetry and music.

Fifteen Essential Canadian Poems in English
by Todd Swift

Those living south of the U.S.–Canadian border may be surprised to discover so many talented Canadian poets of real power and range, writing in such close proximity. In this selection of fifteen Canadian poems that every American should read, I begin with Canada's great Imagist poet, W. W. E. Ross, and end with poets born in the mid- to late 1960s. Along the way, I have selected several of our most famous poems and poets; I've also included a few surprises and offbeat options. As all poetry readers know, the closer one gets to one's own time, the more difficult it is to tell the momentarily thrilling from the infinitely rewarding.

Canadian poetry came to prominence in the 1960s, as did a second wave of feminism, and Margaret Atwood, of course, was a key figure in this regard. With my selections I have tried to represent the degree to which Canadian poetry has been shaped by, and engaged with, women.

To choose from the thousands of Canadian poems I love and admire, I have also considered poems that have been consistently anthologized over several generations; prize-winning poems; and poems that—as far as this is possible—have a claim on posterity. I wanted to consider contemporary poems alongside poems from decades back. I hoped to find a relative balance in region and gender, but this could not be my only governing criteria. To leave room for others equally deserving of a wider readership, I left out work by poets already widely published or read beyond Canada (such as Anne Carson, Daryl Hine, and A. F. Moritz).

Canadians have a centuries-old canon of poetry, in English and French, that is better known at home than abroad. Of the major English-language poets who have become indispensable to world readers, few have come from places other than the United States or the British and Irish archipelago, and those who have done so (one thinks of Derek Walcott or Les Murray) have been published in New York or London and sanctioned by leading critics and poets from these larger "empires" of taste. Perhaps surprisingly, this is not of major concern in Canada. Canadians do not overmuch strive to embrace the main currents of British/Irish poetry; few Canadian poets seek publication beyond their own borders, in foreign magazines, or with larger presses.

This has led to a poetry that relies on plain-spoken anecdotal free verse—a moderate version of William Carlos Williams. As in the U.S., this sort of down-to-earth poem is strongly opposed by a radical, linguistically innovative poetics that follows on from such figures as Charles Olson and Robin Blaser and, radiating predominantly from British Columbia and Ontario, finds international allies among the Oulipo and Language poets. As a result, the traditional, formal poem has been left a little on the back burner. Only in Anglo-Quebec and the Maritimes does an interest in the lyric poem, drawn from the British/Irish tradition, tend to find a foothold, but as these are not the dominant publishing or cultural centers, the "Canadian grain" is drawn mainly west of Montreal. This means that far fewer Canadian poems are going to read as if their makers had ingested large doses of Auden, Larkin, Hughes, Hill, Mahon, or Muldoon, let alone Heaney. Nor are many contemporary Canadian poets expressly influenced by earlier modernists such as Yeats, Eliot, or Stevens.

Indeed, for much of the twentieth century, Canadian artists and writers struggled to define what was uniquely Canadian in a vast country whose main resources were natural and whose people were scattered; a sense of provincial belatedness hung over what was achieved in painting, music, and poetry, until the 1940s at least, by which time Canadian culture made great leaps outward, with international figures such as Marshall MacLuhan, Northrop Frye,

Glenn Gould, Irving Layton, Mordecai Richler, Leonard Cohen, Joni Mitchell, Neil Young, and later David Cronenberg, Celine Dion, Keanu Reeves, Ryan Gosling, and Justin Bieber.

This hodgepodge of names might seem faintly comical in its eclecticism, but it showcases what Canadians admire most in their household names: they must succeed abroad—hopefully in the U.S. first—but never leave home without their Maple Leaf tattoo emblazoned, if only invisibly, on their secret Canadian hearts.

Since 2005, a number of ambitious Canadian literary anthologies have been published in Canada, the United States, and the United Kingdom. These have not been able to achieve a consensus as to what the Great Canadian poem might be or look like: unlike any other major poetry nation, Canada seems to have few bona fide classics that everyone knows by heart or can point to. The contemporary poets who do have broader critical and popular appeal include George Elliott Clarke, Anne Compton, Anne Carson, Mary Dalton, David McGimpsey, Elise Patridge, and Christian Bök, which is indicative of the ongoing heterogeneity of Canadian poetry, as these poets share few if any similarities in poetics, voice, or style.

Other poets who receive near-universal critical approval (at least within Canada) include Margaret Atwood, Al Purdy, P. K. Page, and Michael Ondaatje; these four are in some ways the cornerstones of contemporary Canadian poetry. To this list should be added Leonard Cohen, the nation's troubadour. Of the earlier modernist period, perhaps only A. M. Klein remains consistently impressive, and his reach continues to grow. The reputations of a few once-celebrated poets, including Alden Nowlan, Irving Layton, and Milton Acorn, have withered somewhat; like Dylan Thomas, their colorful lives and dramatic lyric poems, relying heavily on a public persona of excess, keep them both remembered and somewhat suspect among younger readers and poets.

Note: I am indebted to my coeditor Evan Jones; during our work together on Modern Canadian Poets: An Anthology *(Carcanet, 2010), we wrote and researched many poetic biographies together and debated some of these poets and poems; I have drawn on our discussion and anthology in a few instances. All the selections, however, are my own, as are the critical judgments offered—as are any unintended faults.*

~

The essays, novels, stories, and poems of **Margaret Atwood** (born 1939) have made her the defining literary figure of her generation, and beyond. **"Death of a Young Son by Drowning,"** published in 1970, is very much an Atwood poem, with its clipped, almost deadpan tone, its startling use of metaphor and simile (somewhat prefiguring the Martian school of poetry, in England), and its interest in the experience of the newcomer to a wilderness; while nominally about Canada's history of European settlement, the experience of any vulnerable person in an inhospitable setting has appealed to Atwood across her work. In "Death of a Young Son by Drowning" there are two such persons—the young, exhausted mother and the drowned son, the "reckless adventurer," who ends up being "planted" in the new land "like a flag." The irony here is pointed: though the child will not return like a perennial, the political founding of the nation is made of the compost of human loss and suffering. The poem partakes of a key trope in Canadian poetry, that of the swimmer or diver, who seeks to master the turbulent depths (see W.W.E. Ross's "The Diver").

~

I might have selected "The Swimmer's Moment" by **Margaret Avison** (1918-2007) to further the swimming theme but have instead opted for her sonnet **"Snow,"** which has one of the best opening lines in Canadian poetry: "Nobody stuffs the world in at your eyes." Indeed, the image of vision and looking is also a key trope in Canadian poetry (see Anne Wilkinson's "Lens"). Stylish, witty, and eloquent, Avison's spiritual poem is deeply embedded in the material world, reminding us that for the Canadian poet, the exterior world's pressing demands call for internal resources in lush counterbalance.

~

The book-length poem *Eunoia* by **Christian Bök** (born 1966) is perhaps the major long poem of the past two decades in Canadian poetry. Following the Oulipo model, he writes poetic chapters each using only words that employ a particular vowel. What might in some hands be a purely mathematical arrangement becomes out-rageously funny and imaginatively satisfying despite—and because of—its constraints. In the past, avant-garde Canadian poetry has appealed primarily to an elite readership, but this bravura collection has become a relative bestseller. In the process, Bök's experimental vigor has inspired a generation of younger poets.

~

Diana Brebner, who died in her mid-forties (1956–2001), is a poet whose work often grounds its transcendence in the immanent world of suffering and experience. Like Bronwen Wallace, another Canadian poet who died relatively young and has since become influential, Brebner represents a great loss of talent in mid-career. Brebner's **"Port,"** an example of a feminist line that has been such an important part of Canadian poetry since at least the 1960s, builds on her deceptively calm, ordinary language to tell a story of pain: the speaker's surgeon removes the port inset into her body for chemotherapy in an emergency procedure without anesthetic. The speaker must imagine herself elsewhere to cope. The poem echoes A. M. Klein's "Portrait of the Poet as Landscape" (also included here), another poem that presents a lost, suffering poet who must use imagination to survive.

~

George Elliott Clarke (born 1960) received the nation's highest civilian honor, the Order of Canada, in 2008. Descended from African American refugees who fled to the British side in the War of 1812, his major work is the 1990 collection *Whylah Falls,* a sort of Edgar Lee Masters take on small-town Canada. One of the most often anthologized poems from this highly allusive, biblical, multi-vocal book, **"Monologue for Selah Bringing Spring to Whylah Falls"** is a kind of list poem, with something of the sensuous detail of Whitman ("To spy the river crocheted with apple blossoms"). However, this is also a poem about the experience of being black in Canada, in language—"But my lies lie. My colleged speech ripens before you / Becomes Negro-natural, those green, soiled words"—that places the poem in a post-colonial context of work by Derek Walcott and Benjamin Zephaniah. The poem also follows in the working-class English tradition of Tony Harrison. Clarke is a political poet as well as a poet of desire and place. The dramatic exuberance of this poem, especially its inspired ending, paved the way for much performance poetry after it: "Selah, I am bust right upside the head with love!"

~

Over the past decade or so, **Mary Dalton** (born 1950) has become recognized as one of Canada's major living poets, and she has introduced a new tone into the canon. As in the unconventional sonnet **"Flirrup,"** much of the charm and pleasure of her work is in the mingling of linguistic ingenuity and recourse to the speech patterns of Newfoundland, where she was born and which has Catholic and Celtic roots that make it in some ways a culture as unique as Quebec's. Dalton has established a viable contemporary line back to the fecundity of Irish poetry, with its rootedness in place, people, and passion, and of course, finally, in the music of poetic expression.

~

"The Machine Gunner" by Stephen Heighton (born 1961) deals with a common Canadian theme, World War 1, and describes the harrowing experience of a Canadian machine gunner faced with the German enemy approaching "like a file of mourners" into gaps in the barbed wire. As he holds his fire, almost benevolently, these men run towards him, and he sees the opposing soldiers in a more positive light: boys "rushing towards us with arms outstretched," with their hands "clenched as if in urgent prayer." Finally the gunner perceives them as children hurrying forward to be rescued. The final three lines in this poem are amongst the most chilling and brutal in Canadian poetry. Their terse rapidity and violence break a taboo by exposing the small-town Canadian soldier not as a figure of eternal virtue and decency but of small-minded belligerence, exposing a deeper truth about the unheroic nature of war.

~

A. M. Klein (1909–1972), Canadian modernism's preeminent poet, was a visionary, inspired to form a hybrid language derived from the traditions of Shakespeare and James Joyce and from Jewish and francophone culture. No other Canadian poet of the period uses language in such a richly diverse and original way. Klein is intellectual, sentimental, and syntactically complex in the same verse; like other great 1940s poets, he sought a romanticism that was also classically informed. Klein, who died in Montreal in 1972, suffered from mental illness for decades. His collection *The Rocking Chair and Other Poems* (1948) has claim to be the best single volume by a Canadian, in terms of its uniform excellence. "Portrait of the

Poet as Landscape" is Klein's magisterial, rambunctious, screwball, and tormented elegy for the poet absent from any central role in modern society. In six sections and 162 lines, he explores how the poet, "like the corpse in a detective novel" may be "dead, and not discovered" or "beyond recognition lost in love." By turns mournful and funny, the poem takes inventory of ways in which poets can self-destruct or become lost ("sick with sex," "everywhere menial, a shadow's shadow"); the poem also counts the ways a poet can make of "his status as a zero a rich garland," can make of his anonymity a halo, shining like phosphorous "at the bottom of the sea."

~

David McGimpsey (born 1962) has brought something new to Canadian poetry. This most pro-"pop culture" of all Canadian poets has mapped a wacky landscape larded with fast food, sitcoms, and Americana, a space often enjoyed and narrated by a Canadian mediating presence. McGimpsey's work is located at the intersection between the bluntly local—in his case Anglophone working-class Montreal—and the international capitalist realm of entertainment that is located precisely nowhere and everywhere at once. Many poets before McGimpsey have written poems about television, rock 'n roll, and hamburgers, of course—David Trinidad in the U.S. comes to mind as one sort of corollary. McGimpsey, however, is unique: his poetics is informed by the traditional canon but is equally open to the extremely contemporary cultural artifacts of the past fifty years. When McGimpsey writes about Las Vegas, or Starbucks, or in the featured poem's instance, *Gilligan's Island*, a favorite childhood TV program, he isn't being ironic, or hip, or sneeringly sarcastic. There is a reverence for these fictional characters. In one of the key passages in recent Canadian poetry, McGimpsey's long poem **"In Memoriam: A. H. Jr."** (modeled on Tennyson's great "In Memoriam") asserts that "Saying it was only a TV show / is like saying it was only a friend, / only my brother, only my father." This startling claim, in iambic pentameter, that television forms a bond as imperative as the familial is genuinely moving, despite its gloss of the postmodern. McGimpsey doesn't look down on the media world he surveys but rather, immersed entirely within it, he freely engages with its creative possibilities.

~

Joan Murray (1918–1942) is of ambiguous nationality: Canadians, Americans, and the British have claimed her as their own. Her parents were Canadian but she was born in London and mostly raised in the U.S. with a brief stint in Ontario. In this sense, she is very much a Canadian poet—rendered nearly invisible due to competing cultural interests. She is Canada's missing link with the New York School of poetry and with an entire poetic style not often associated with Canada—abstract lyricism. Influenced by W. H. Auden, Murray in turn was an influence on, among others, John Ashbery, who has written of her "whirlwind trajectories." Her modernist, playful, strange syntax is much in evidence in **"Even The Gulls of the Cool Atlantic."**

~

Richard Outram (1930–2005) committed suicide, two years after his wife died during a routine operation, by simply going onto the porch of his house in Port Hope in the winter and letting the elements have their way with him. He is one of Canada's more tragic poets, not least because this witty, brilliant man, who spent time working for the BBC in London and studied with Northrop Frye, has become curiously neglected—a poet's poet whose advocates are a clutch of discerning poets and critics. Outram was a master formalist whose poems are often witty and metaphysical. **"Barbed Wire"** is as perfect a short lyric poem as a Canadian has ever written, and, like Steven Heighton's poem "The Machine Gunner," uses war imagery. What distinguishes Outram's five-quatrain poem, with its ABAB rhyme scheme, is the mastery of the emotional and imagistic arguments, which intertwine. The first three lines are worthy of Donne: [Barbed wire] "Consists of two tight-twisted, separate strands / Conjoined as one: and not unlike, in fact / Our own familiar silver wedding bands." This description flows into a discussion of marriage and his father's wartime experience before culminating in the final brilliance of the last lines: "They stood, to view / Our brief exchange of rings and vows, for both / Our fathers had survived the war: and knew / Of death, and bright entanglement, and troth."

⌣

P. K. Page (1916–2010) has claim to be as fine a poet as Elizabeth Bishop, and by many is considered Canada's greatest twentieth-century poet, in terms of her range and sustained quality of creation. She lived in both Brazil and Japan (her husband was in the diplomatic corps), and she painted along with writing; earlier in her career, she had been associated with the Montreal Preview group of A. M. Klein, F. R. Scott, and Patrick Anderson. In a great leap of poetic fancy, **"After Rain"** takes the quotidian backyard of a "housewife," as it were, and transforms this, via the imagination, into a "pure line." Page does so in a sequence of extraordinary images. The poem opens with "The snails have made a garden of green lace: broderie anglaise from the cabbages," which Page calls "female whimsy." As in other key Canadian poems, the challenges of poetic vocation and vision come to the fore, as here, where Page calls out: "And choir me too to keep my heart a size / Larger than seeing, unseduced by each / Bright glimpse of beauty striking like a bell."

⌣

W. W. E. Ross (1894–1966) is now a marginal figure to many Canadians, and yet in the 1920s and 1930s he was one of the few

Canadian poets to engage actively with the modernist tradition
of Ezra Pound and the work of Max Jacob, which he translated.
Ross's poem **"The Diver"** is one of the first imagist-style poems
written in Canada, and also inaugurates a particular sub-genre
of Canadian poetry, the poem about diving into a body of water;
Canada of course is a country with thousands of lakes and rivers
as well as being bounded on three sides by seas. Canadian poems
(as seen with the Atwood and Avison selections) often explore the
process of breaking a surface and going beneath natural elemental
spaces, sometimes in an acquiescent way, at other times as an act
of will, a gesture of defiance. In "The Diver," the water is hostile
and the rocks are "slime-covered," yet the rocks at the bottom are
"safely deep" so there is a zone of comfort within the "green glim-
mer." Finally, though, the diver—who is also the poet—must return
after his creative immersion into what Ross describes as "the light/
White and ordinary of the day."

David Wevill is arguably the best Canadian poet of the twentieth
century to remain a kind of invisible man, although (or because) he
is one of the most international in outlook and experience, hav-
ing lived in Japan (where he was born in 1935 of Canadian parents),
England, and for many years the United States. To make things
more frustrating for those who admire his work, despite being
closely associated with Sylvia Plath and Ted Hughes (his wife was
Assia Wevill, the second Mrs. Hughes) and with the circle of influ-
ential British poets in the Group, he is now not often read in that
context. This is somewhat related to a certain peculiarly English
chauvinism, in some critical circles; for, although Wevill's poems
were widely published in Britain, including by Penguin in their key
series of the time, and he had been a student at Cambridge, once he
left in 1968, he seemed to have never been there at all. Wevill's early
collections are marked by a brilliant formal rigor. *A Christ of the Ice*

Floes (1966) was a finalist, alongside Margaret Atwood's debut of that year, for Canada's Governor General's Literary Award for Poetry or Drama. Had it won, the history of Canadian poetry might be very different, having taken a path less shy of British influences; instead, the long Canadian exclusion of many fine anglocentric stylists began (think of John Glassco, Daryl Hine, and Jay Macpherson—in Canada these are thought to be eccentrics, yet if read in the light of British poetry, they suddenly sound central). This is the argument known as cosmopolitanism in Canadian letters, and its repudiation in the 1970s in his homeland was the main reason that Wevill's work has been less studied than it should be. Since 1994 a dual citizen of Canada and the U.S., Wevill has endured a sort of long exile in Texas, where he has taught for many years at the university in Austin. This poet is always good at exploring the objective correlatives nature and landscape—one of his great poems is about the birth of a shark—with an always nuanced balance between confessionalism and impersonal, modernist details. The achingly sad, deeply allusive **"Diamonds"** shows him at his best.

~

Anne Wilkinson (1910–1961) started writing her macabre poems in the 1940s and attended poetry readings where she would have seen and heard A. M. Klein and W. W. E. Ross. **"Lens"** is a discomfiting, visionary poem, with staccato lines and surprising claims: "The poet's daily chore / Is my daily duty; / To keep and cherish my good lens / For love and war / And wasps about the lilies / And mutiny within." Wilkinson has something of the eccentric modesty of Emily Dickinson here, and also has Dickinson's vibrant metaphoric insight, as the "lens," which is both camera and viscous eye, confronts death "in black and white."

Suggestions for Further Reading

〜

GHANA

In addition to individual collections of poems by Ama Ata Aidoo, Kofi Awoonor, Kofi Anyidoho, Kwesi Brew, Abena Busia, Frank Kobina Parkes, Nii Parkes, Atukwei Okai, and Efua Sutherland, curator Kwame Dawes recommends the following anthologies.

African Poetry: An Anthology of Traditional African Poetry, edited by Ulli Beier (Cambridge University Press, 1966).

Bending the Bow: An Anthology of African Love Poetry, edited by Frank Chipasula (Southern Illinois University Press, 2009).

Echoes of the Sunbird: An Anthology of Contemporary African Poetry, edited by Don Burness (Ohio RIS Africa Series, Ohio University Press, 1993).

Messages: Poems from Ghana, edited by Kofi Awoonor and G. Adali Mortty (African Writers Series, Longman, 1971).

The New African Poetry: An Anthology, edited by Tanure Ojaide and Tijan M. Sallah, (Three Continents Press, 1999).

The Penguin Book of Modern African Poetry, edited by Gerald Moore and Ulli Beier (Penguin Classics, 2007).

West African Poetry: A Critical History, by Robert Fraser (Cambridge University Press, 1986).

〜

CARIBBEAN

Ishion Hutchinson recommends the following books by Caribbean poets.

Edward Baugh, *Black Sand: New and Selected Poems* (Peepal Tree Press, 2013).

Andre Bagoo, *Trick Vessels* (Shearsman Books, 2012).

Louise Bennett, *Selected Poems*, edited by Mervyn Morris (Sangster's Book Stores, 1982).

Dionne Brand, *No Language is Neutral* (McClelland & Stewart, 1998).

Edward Kamau Brathwaite, *Arrivants: A New World Trilogy — Rights of Passage / Islands / Masks* (Oxford University Press, 1988).

Jean "Binta" Breeze, *On the Edge of an Island* (Bloodaxe Books, 1997).

Wayne Brown, *On the Coast and Other Poems* (Peepal Tree Press, 2011).

Vahni Capildeo, *Undraining Sea* (Egg Box Publishing, 2009).

Christian Campbell, *Running the Dusk* (Peepal Tree Press, 2010).

Merle Collins, *Lady in a Boat* (Peepal Tree Press, 2003).

Frank Collymore, *Collected Poems* (Advocate, 1959).

Fred D'Aguiar, *Continental Shelf* (Carcanet, 2011).

David Dabydeen, *Turner: New and Selected Poems* (Peepal Tree Press, 2002).

Mahadai Das, *A Leaf in His Ear: Selected Poems* (Peepal Tree Press, 2010).

Kwame Dawes, *Duppy Conqueror: New and Selected Poems* (Copper Canyon Press, 2013).

Neville Dawes, *Fugue and Other Poems* (Peepal Tree Press, 2008).

Gloria Escoffery, *Mother Jackson Murders the Moon* (Peepal Tree Press, 1998).

John Figueroa, *The Chase* (Peepal Tree Press, 1992).

Lorna Goodison, *Guinea Woman: New and Selected Poems* (Carcanet Press, 2001).

Wilson Harris, *Eternity to Season* (New Beacon Books, 1979).

Kendel Hippolyte, *Fault Lines* (Peepal Tree Press, 2012).

Linton Kwesi Johnson, *Dread Beat and Blood* (Bogle L'Overture Press, 1975).

Jane King, *Fellow Travellers* (Sandberry Press, 1994).

John Robert Lee, *Elemental: New and Selected Poems* (Peepal Tree Press, 2008).

Claude McKay, *The Passion of Claude McKay: Selected Prose and Poetry, 1912–1948* (Knopf, 1976).

Rachel Manley, *A Light Left On* (Peepal Tree Press, 1991).

E. A. Markham, *Rough Climate* (Anvil Press, 2004).

Anthony McNeil, *Chinese Lanterns for the Blue Child* (Peepal Tree Press, 1998).

Mark McWatt, *The Language of El Dorado* (Dangeroo Press, 1994).

Kei Miller, *A Light Song of Light* (Carcanet Press, 2010).

Mervyn Morris, *I Been There, Sort Of: New and Selected Poems* (Carcanet Press, 2006).

Grace Nichols, *I Is a Long Memoried Woman* (Karnak House Publishers, 1983).

Velma Pollard, *And Caret Bay Again: New and Selected Poems* (Peepal Tree Press, 2013).

Jennifer Rahim, *Approaching Sabbaths* (Peepal Tree Press, 2013).

Claudia Rankine, *Nothing in Nature is Private* (Cleveland State University Center, 1995).

Dennis Scott, *After-Image* (Peepal Tree Press, 2008).

Olive Senior, *Gardening in the Tropics* (Bloodaxe Books, 1995).

M. G. Smith, *In the Kingdom of Light: Collected Poems* (The Mill Press, 2003).

Derek Walcott, *Collected Poems: 1948-1984* (Farrar, Straus and Giroux, 1987).

~

SOUTH AFRICA

Rustum Kozain recommends a selection of anthologies covering modern and contemporary South African poetry.

The Lava of This Land: South African Poetry, 1960-1996, edited by Denis Hirson (TriQuarterly Books, 1997).

The New Century of South African Poetry, edited by Michael Chapman and Achmat Dangor (Ad Donker, 2002).

The Return of the Amasi Bird: Black South African Poetry 1891-1981, edited by Tim Couzens and Essop Patel (Ravan Press, 1982).

Soweto Poetry, edited by Michael Chapman (McGraw-Hill, 1982).

Voices from Within: Black Poetry from Southern Africa, edited by Michael Chapman and Achmat Dangor (Johannesburg: Ad Donker, 1982).

Websites (for more recent selections):

The online journal *The Common* (see issue #4) features a selection of recent South African poetry in English, compiled, edited and with an introduction by Kelwyn Sole:

http://www.thecommononline.org/

Poetry International Rotterdam has a gradually expanding selection of South African poetry, including audios and videos, some originally in English and other pieces translated from various other South African language into English:

http://www.poetryinternationalweb.net/pi/site/country/item/10/ South-Africa

~

AOTEAROA/NEW ZEALAND

Hinemoana Baker recommends a selection of books and other resources to further explore the poetry of her region.

Anthologies:

The Best of Best New Zealand Poems, edited by Bill Manhire and Damien Wilkins (Victoria University Press, 2011).

Mauri Ola: Contemporary Polynesian Poems in English, edited by Albert Wendt, Reina Whaitiri, and Robert Sullivan (Auckland University Press, 2010).

Individual collections of poems:

Tusiata Avia, *Blood Clot* (Victoria University Press, 2009).

James K. Baxter, *Selected Poems*, edited by Paul Millar (Carcanet, 2010).

James Brown, *Lemon* (Victoria University Press, 1999).

Geoff Cochrane, *The Bengal Engine's Mango Afterglow* (Victoria University Press, 2012).

Cliff Fell, *The Adulterer's Bible* (Victoria University Press, 2004).

Cilla McQueen, *Soundings* (Otago University Press, 2002).

Karlo Mila, *Dream Fish Floating* (Huia Publishers, 2007).

Christ Price, *Brief Lives* (Auckland University Press, 2007).

Robert Sullivan, *Voice Carried My Family* (Auckland University Press, 2005).

Jo Thorpe, *in/let* (Steele Roberts, 2011).

Nick Twemlow, *Palm Trees* (Green Lantern Press, 2012).

Ian Wedde, *The Lifeguard: New Poems 2008–2013* (Auckland University Press, 2013).

Presses, online publications, and literary journals:

Blackmail Press, an online publisher that presents "a range of voices from Aotearoa and abroad," receptive to emerging poets. www.blackmailpress.com/.

4th Floor, an online literary journal produced by Whitireia Polytechnic. Published annually. www.whitireia.ac.nz/4thfloor/.

JAAM, a literary journal produced by The JAAM Collective. Published annually.

Landfall, a literary journal produced by Otago University Press. Published biannually.

Poetry New Zealand: International Journal of Poetry and Poetics, edited by Alistair Reid and produced by Puriri Press / Brick Row. Published biannually since 1951.

SPORT, a literary journal produced by Victoria University Press. Published biannually.

Tinfish Press, which publishes experimental poetry and prose from the Pacific region. http://Tinfishpress.com/.

Turbine, an online literary journal produced by Victoria University. Published annually. www.victoria.ac.nz/modernletters/resources/turbine/.

Recordings:

Baxter (CD), various artists (Universal Music, 2000).

Tuwhare (CD), various artists (Universal Music, 2005).

～

MODERN INDIAN POETRY, POST-1950

Other publications recommended for readers seeking to further explore Indian poetry in English.

Anthologies:

Another Country: An Anthology of Post-Independence Indian Poetry in English, edited by Arundhathi Subramaniam (Sahitya Akademi, 2013).

Confronting Love, edited by Jerry Pinto and Arundhathi Subramaniam (Penguin, 2005).

The HarperCollins Book of English Poetry, edited by Sudeep Sen (HarperCollins, 2011).

Indian Love Poems, edited by Meena Alexander (Everyman's Library, 2005).

Indivisible: An Anthology of Contemporary South Asian American Poetry, edited by Neelanjana Banerjee, Summi Kaipa, and Pireeni Sundaralingam (University of Arkansas Press, 2010).

Leela: An Erotic Play of Verse and Art, edited Alka Pande (Collins, 2009).

Ten: The New Indian Poets, edited by Jayanta Mahapatra and Yuyutsu Sharma (Nirala, 2013).

These My Words: The Penguin Book of Indian Poetry, edited by Eunice De Souza and Melanie Silgardo (Penguin India, 2012).

Special Issues of Journals:

"Modern English Poetry by Indians," special issue, only online now, edited by Sudeep Sen (*The Yellow Nib*, Issue 6, July 2012). Queen's University, Belfast. See: www.qub.ac.uk/schools/ SeamusHeaneyCentreforPoetry/YellowNib/

"Unmapped: Modern Indian Poetry,"; special issue edited by Sudeep Sen; Minna Proctor, editor. *The Literary Review* (Volume 52, Number 3, Spring 2009), Farleigh Dickinson University.

"Writing from Modern India," special selection edited by Sudeep Sen; Daniel Simon, editor. *World Literature Today* (Volume 84, Number 6, November/December 2010), University of Oklahoma.

Individual Volumes of Poems:

Meena Alexander, *Birthplace with Buried Stones* (Triquarterly Books, 2013).

Kazim Ali, *The Far Mosque* (Alice James Books, 2005).

Sujata Bhatt, *Point No Point: Selected Poems* (Caracanet, 1997).

Imtiaz Dharker, *Postcards from Gods* (Bloodaxe, 1997).

Ranjit Hoskote, *Vanishing Acts: New and Selected Poems, 1985–2005* (Penguin India, 2006).

Deepankar Khiwani, *Entracte* (Harbour Line, 2006).

Amit Majmudar, *0, 0* (Triquarterly Books, 2009).

Taj Masud, *Alphabestiary* (Exile Editions, 2011).

Karthika Nair, *Bearings* (HarperCollins India, 2009).

Rukmini Bhaya Nair, *The Yellow Hibiscus* (Penguin India, 2004).

Aimee Nezhukumatathil, *At the Drive-In Volcano* (Tupelo Press, 2007).

Srikanth Reddy, *Facts for Visitors* (University of California Press, 2004)

Sudeep Sen, *Blue Nude: Selected Poems & Translations* (Partridge/ Penguin Random House, 2014)

Vijay Seshadri, *The Disappearances* (HarperCollins India, 2007).

Ravi Shankar, *Instrumentality* (WordTech Communications, 2004).

Anis Shivani, *My Tranquil War and Other Poems* (New York Quarterly Books, 2012).

C. P. Surendran, *Portraits of the Spaces We Occupy* (HarperCollins India, 2007).

Anand Thakore, *Elephant Bathing: Poems 2001–2011* (Poetrywala).

~

CANADA

Todd Swift recommends "Twenty-one More Great Canadian Poems to Know."

1. A. F. Moritz, "The Snake," from *The New Measures* (House of Anansi, 2012).

2. Alden Nowlan, "Beginning," from *Between Tears and Laughter: Selected Poems* (Bloodaxe, 2004).

3. Amanda Jernigan, "Translations," from *Groundwork* (Bibliosasis, 2011).

4. Anne Carson, "Interview," from *Autobiography of Red* (Cape Poetry / Vintage, 1999).

5. Carmine Starnino, "On The Obsolescence of Caphone," from *With English Subtitles* (Gaspereau Press, 2004).

6. Catherine Graham, "The Buried," from *Winterkill* (Insomniac Press, 2010).

7. Daniel O'Leary, "Of The Decadent Poets," from *The Lower Provinces* (DC Books, 2012).

8. Don McKay, "Precambrian Shield," from *Strike/Slip* (McClelland and Stewart, 2006).

9. Elizabeth Bachinsky, "Drive," from *Home of Sudden Service* (Nightwood Editions, 2006).

10. Eric Ormsby, "Flamingos," from *For A Modest God: New and Selected Poems* (Grove Press, 1997).

11. Jason Camlot, "Natural," from *The Animal Library* (DC Books, 2000).

12. Jason Guriel, "The Hard To Get Rid Of," from *Pure Product* (Signal, 2009).

13. Jay Macpherson, "Phoenix," from *Poems Twice Told: The Boatman and Welcoming Disaster* (Oxford University Press, 1981).

14. John Newlove, "Lady, Lady," from *The Long Continual Argument: The Selected Poems* (Chaudiere Books, 2007).

15. John Thompson, "Stilt Jack," from *I Dream Myself Into Being: Collected Poems* (House of Anansi, 1991).

16. Karen Solie, "Tractor," from *Pigeon* (House of Anansi, 2009).

17. Ken Babstock, "Another Dim Boy Claps," from *Days Into Flatspin* (House of Anansi, 2001).

18. Lisa Robertson, "How To Judge," from *Debbie: An Epic* (New Star Books, 1997).

19. Robert Allen, "The Encantadas," from *The Encantadas* (Conundrum Press, 2006).

20. Sina Queyras, "What Books Our Lives Have Become," from *Teethmarks* (Nightwood Editions, 2004).

21. Stephanie Bolster, "Stuffed Stuff," from *A Page From The Wonders of Life On Earth* (Brick Books, 2011).

Acknowledgments and Permissions

For permission to use previously published and copyrighted work in *Another English*, grateful acknowledgment is made to the following persons, organizations, and companies. Details of these acknowledgments are as supplied by the copyright-holders. Any questions regarding the contents of this book should be addressed to Tupelo Press.

Aboud, James Christopher: "Wind, Water, Fire, Men," from *Lagahoo Poems* (Peepal Tree Press, 2007). Reprinted with permission of the publisher.

Afrika, Tatamkhulu: "Dark Rider," from *Nightrider: Selected Poems* (Kwela Boeke/Snailpress, 2004). Copyright © 2004 Tatamkhulu Afrika. Reprinted by permission of the Proprietor.

Aidoo, Ama Ata: "Totems." Previously published in *The Heinemann Book of African Women's Poetry* (Heinemann, 1995) and *The Penguin Book of Modern African Poetry* (Penguin, 2007). Reprinted with permission of the poet.

Annobil, Ishmael Fiifi: "Rwanda," from *Seven Horn Elegy* (Totem, 1998). Copyright © 1998 Fiifi Ayerebi Annobil. Reprinted with permission of the poet (see http://annobil.photoshelter.com/ and www.chiaroscuromagazine.com/).

Anyidoho, Kofi: "Doctrine & Ethics," from *Praise Song for the Land: Poems of Hope and Love* (Sub-Saharan Publishers, Accra, 2002). Copyright © 2002 Kofi Anyidoho. Reprinted with permission of the poet.

Atwood, Margaret: "Death of a Young Son by Drowning," included by permission of the author and Houghton Mifflin Harcourt Publishing Company. All rights reserved. Available in the following collections: In the United States, *Selected Poems I, 1965–1975*, copyright © 1976 by Margaret Atwood (Houghton Mifflin, 1976); in Canada, *Selected Poems, 1966–1984*, copyright 1990 Margaret Atwood (Oxford University Press, 1990); in the United Kingdom and British Commonwealth, *Eating Fire*, copyright 1998 Margaret Atwood (Virago Books, 1998).

Avia, Tusiata: "Wild Dogs Under My Skirt," from *Wild Dogs Under My Skirt* (Victoria University Press, 2004). Copyright © 2004 Tusiata Avia. Reprinted with permission of the poet.

Avison, Margaret: "Snow," previously published in *Always Now: Collected Poems of Margaret Avison* (in three volumes, The Porcupine's Quill, 2003) and *The Essential Margaret Avison*, selected by Robyn Sarah (The Porcupine's Quill, 2010). Copyright 2010 the Estate of Margaret Avison. Reprinted with permission of the publisher.

Awoonor, Kofi: "My God of Songs Was Ill," "Sea Time," and "The Weaver Bird," previously published in *Until the Morning After: Collected Poems 1963–1985* (Greenfield Review Press, 1987; co-published in Ghana by Woeli Publishers), and then in *The Promise of Hope: New and Selected Poems, 1964–2013* (University of Nebraska Press, 2014). Copyright © by the Board of Regents of the University of Nebraska Press. Reprinted with permission of the poet's family and the University of Nebraska Press.

Baugh, Edward: "The Carpenter's Complaint," first published in *A Tale from the Rainforest* (Sandberry Press, 1988) and republished in *It Was the Singing* (Sandberry Press, 2000) is used with permission of the poet and Sandberry Press.

Bethel, Marion: excerpts from "In the Marketplace," from *Bougainvillea Ringplay* (Peepal Tree Press, 2009). Reprinted with permission of the publisher.

Bök, Christian: excerpts from *Eunoia* (first edition: Coach House Books, 2001; upgraded edition: Coach House Books, 2009). Copyright © 2001 Christian Bök. Reprinted with permission of the poet and the publisher.

Bornholdt, Jenny: "Wedding Song," from *How We Met* (Victoria University Press, 1995). Copyright © 1995 Jenny Bornholdt. Reprinted with permission of the poet.

Brand, Dionne: section "XII" excerpted from "Land to Light On," from *Land to Light On* (McClelland & Stewart, 1997). Copyright © 1997 by Dionne Brand. Reprinted with permission of The Wylie Agency LLC (electronic rights) and McClelland & Stewart (print-edition rights).

Brathwaite, Kamau: excerpt from "Stone," from *Middle Passages* (New Directions, 1993). Copyright © 1993 Kamau Brathwaite. Reprinted with permission of New Directions Publishing Corporation.

Brebner, Diana: "Port," from *The Ishtar Gate: Last and Selected Poems* (McGill-Queen's University Press, 2005). Copyright © 2005 the Estate of Diana Brebner. Reprinted with permission of the publisher.

Brew, Kwesi: "Adam and Eve and the New Paradise," from *Return of No Return and Other Poems* (Afram Publications Ltd., Ghana, 1995). Reprinted with permission of the publisher.

Brown, James: "No Rest," from *The Year of the Bicycle* (Victoria University Press, 2006). Copyright © 2006 James Brown. Reprinted with permission of the poet.

Busia, Abena: "Caliban," from *Testimonies of Exile* (Africa World Press, New Jersey, 1990). Copyright © 1990 Abena P. A. Busia. Reprinted with permission of the publisher.

Cahill, Michelle: "Kali from Abroad" and "The Piano Lesson" from *Vishvarupa* (Five Islands Press, 2011). Reprinted with permission of the poet (http://michellecahill.com/).

Camp, Kate: "Snow White's Coffin," from *Snow White's Coffin* (Victoria University Press, 2013). Copyright © 2013 Kate Camp. Reprinted with permission of the poet.

Campbell, Christian: "Iguana," from *Running the Dusk* (Peepal Tree Press, 2010). Reprinted with permission of the publisher.

Campbell, Meg: "Silly," from *Dear Heart: 150 New Zealand Love Poems*, edited by Paula Green (Godwit, 2012). Copyright © 2012 the Estate of Meg Campbell. Reprinted with permission of the poet's family.

Capildeo, Vahni: Segment "Light and Dark" from "Time is an Unkind Dancer," from *No Traveler Returns* (Salt Publishing, 2003). Copyright © 2003 Vahni Capildeo. Reprinted with permission of the poet.

Carter, Martin: "Proem," from *University of Hunger: Collected Poems and Selected Prose*, edited by Gemma Robinson (Bloodaxe Books, 2006). Reprinted with permission of the publisher.

Chabria, Priya Sarukkai: "Everyday Things in My Life," previously published in *The Literary Review* (special issue on Indian writing; Spring 2009: volume 52, Issue 3) and in *The HarperCollins Book of English Poetry*, edited by Sudeep Sen (HarperCollins Publishers India, 2011). Reprinted with permission of the poet (http://priyawriting.com/).

Chaudhuri, Amit: "Insomniac" and "The Writers" previously published in *The HarperCollins Book of English Poetry*, edited by Sudeep Sen (HarperCollins Publishers India, 2011). Reprinted with permission of the poet (http://www.amitchaudhuri.com/).

Clarke, George Elliott: "Monologue for Selah Bringing Spring to Whylah Falls," from *Whylah Falls* (Gaspereau Press, 2010). Reprinted with permission of the poet and publisher.

Compton, Jennifer: "From the other woman left under the pillow," from *The Other Woman* (Five Islands New Poets Series, Scarp Press, 1993). Reprinted with permission of the poet (see www.otago.ac.nz/press/Thiscityjennifercompton.html).

Coverdale, Tom: "Woodwind," previously published in the journal *Quadrant* (Australia; 2004), then in *The Best Australian Poems 2005*, edited by Les Murray (Black Inc., 2005). Reprinted with permission of the poet.

Cronin, Jeremy: "[To learn how to speak]" and an excerpt from "Walking on Air," from *Inside* (Ravan Press, Johannesburg; 1983; Cape, London; 1987); and "Running Toward Us," from *Even the Dead: Poems, Parables & a Jeremiad* (Bellville: Mayibuye Books and Cape Town: David Philip Publishers, 1997). Reprinted with permission of the poet.

D'Aguiar, Fred: "Demerara Sugar," from *Continental Shelf* (Carcanet Press, 2009). Reprinted with permission of the publisher.

Dalton, Mary: "Flirrup," from *Merrybegot* (Véhicule Press, 2003). Reprinted with permission of Signal Editions/Véhicule Press and the poet.

Das, Mahadai: "They Came in Ships," previously published in *The Oxford Book of Caribbean Verse*, edited by Stewart Browne and Mark McWatt (Oxford University Press, 2005), and more recently in *A Leaf in His Ear: Selected Poems* (Peepal Tree, 2010). Reprinted with permission of Peepal Tree Press.

Davidson, Lynn: "How to live by the sea," from *How to Live by the Sea* (Victoria University Press, 2009). Copyright © 2009 Lynn Davidson. Reprinted with permission of the poet.

Dawes, Kwame: "Yap," from *Progeny of Air* (Peepal Tree Press, 1994); also in *Duppy Conquerer: New and Selected Poems* (Copper Canyon Press, 2013). Reprinted with permission of Peepal Tree Press.

Gray, Robert: "Among the Mountains of Guang-xi Province in Southern China," from *Daylight Saving: A Selection of Poems* (Australian Poets Series, George Braziller, 2013). Copyright © 2013 Robert Gray. Reprinted by permission of George Braziller, Inc. All rights reserved.

Hall, Bernadette: "duck," from *the merino princess: selected poems* (Victoria University Press, 2004). Copyright © 2004Bernadette Hall. Reprinted with permission of the poet.

Harford, Lesbia: "[I'm like all lovers]," from *Hell and After: Four Early English-Language Poets of Australia*, edited by Les Murray (Carcanet / ETT Imprint, 2005). Reprinted with permission of ETT Imprint.

Harvey, Margaret: "Living in M—LS&B—N," previously published in the journal *Quadrant* (2004), and in *The Best Australian Poems 2004*, edited by Les Murray (Black Inc., 2004). Reprinted with permission of the poet's family.

Heighton, Steven: "The Machine Gunner," from *The Ecstasy of Skeptics* (House of Anansi Press, 1994). Reprinted with permission of the publisher.

Hippolyte, Kendel: "Night Vision," previously in *Night Vision* (Northwestern University Press, 2005), and forthcoming in *Night Vision* (Peepal Tree Press, 2014). Reprinted with permission of Peepal Tree Press.

Hodgins, Philip: "Midday Horizon," from *Selected Poems* (Angus & Robertson, 1997). Reprinted with permission of HarperCollins Australia.

Horn, Peter: "The Fourth Elegy," from the series "The Plumstead Elegies" originally published in *Silence in Jail* (Scribe Press, 1979: banned until 1991), and now in *Poems 1964–2010* (Peter Horn, 2011). Reprinted with permission of the poet (http://peterhorn.kilu.de/peterhome.htm).

Jenner, Lynn: "When I had a son in his early teens," previously unpublished. Reprinted with permission of the poet.

Kayper-Mensah, A. W.: "Dying Birth," from *The Drummer in Our Time* (Heinemann Educational, 1975). Copyright © 1975 A. W. Kayper-Mensah. Reprinted with permission of Pearson Education Limited.

McGimpsey, David: "In Memoriam: A. H. Jr.," from *Lardcake* (ECW Press, 1996). Reprinted with permission of the publisher.

McKay, Claude: "If We Must Die," first published in published in *The Liberator Magazine* (1919), then in the book *Harlem Shadows: The Poems of Claude McKay* (Harcourt, Brace and Co., 1922). This poem is now in the public domain.

McNeill, Anthony: "Hello Ungod," from the book *Reel from "The Life Movie"* (Savacou Publications, 1972). Reprinted with permission of Peepal Tree Press.

Miller, Kei: "Some Definitions for Light," from *A Light Song of Light* (Carcanet, 2010). Reprinted with permission of the publisher.

Morgan - Shae, Ashlley: "Edinburgh," previously published in the journals *Quadrant* (Australia; 2006) and *The Reader* (University of Liverpool, U.K.; Autumn 2008). Copyright © 2006 Ashlley Morgan - Shae. Reprinted with permission of the poet (http://ashlleymorganshae.com).

Morris, Mervyn: "Peelin' Oranges," from *I been there, sort of: New and Selected Poems* (Carcanet, 2006). Reprinted with permission of the publisher.

Murray, Joan: "Even the Gulls of the Cool Atlantic," from *Poems* (Yale Series of Younger Poets, selected by W. H. Auden; Yale University Press, 1947). Reprinted with permission of the Sophia Smith Collection, Smith College, where the Joan and Peggy Murray Papers are now archived.

Nortje, Arthur: "Native's Letter," from *Anatomy of Dark: The Collected Poems of Arthur Nortje* (Unisa Press, 2000). Reprinted with permission of the publisher.

Okai, Atukwei: "Watu Wazuri," previously published in *FonTomFrom: Contemporary Ghanaian Literature, Theatre and Film*, edited by Kofi Anyidoho and James Gibbs (Editions Rodopi B.V., 2000). Reprinted with permission of the poet.

Oliphant, Andries Walter: "Childhood in Heidelberg," from *At the End of the Day* (Bellevue East/Justified Press, 1988). Reprinted with permission of the poet.

Opoku-Agyemang, Kwadwo: "In the Dungeon" and "Cape Coast Town," previously published in *FonTomFrom: Contemporary Ghanaian Literature, Theatre and Film*, edited by Kofi Anyidoho and James Gibbs (Editions Rodopi B.V., 2000). Reprinted with permission of the poet.

Outram, Richard: "Barbed Wire," from *Dove Legend & Other Poems* (The Porcupine Quill, 2001), and from *The Essential Richard Outram*, selected by Amanda Jernigan (The Porcupine's Quill, 2011). Copyright © 2011 the Estate of Richard Outram. Reprinted with permission of the publisher.

Page, P. K.: "After Rain," from *Planet Earth: Poems, Selected and New* (The Porcupine's Quill, 2002), and from *The Essential P. K. Page*, selected by Arlene Lampert and Théa Gray (The Porcupine's Quill, 2008). Copyright © 2008 the Estate of P. K. Page. Reprinted with permission of the publisher.

Parmar, Sandeep: "Counsel" and "Invocation," from *The Marble Orchard* (Shearsman Books, 2012). Copyright © 2012 Sandeep Parmar. Used with permission of the poet and the publisher.

Philip, M. NourbeSe: "Discourse on the Logic of Language," from *She Tries Her Tongue, Her Silence Softly Breaks* (Poui Publications, 2005). Copyright © 1989 M. NourbeSe Philip. Reprinted with permission of the poet (http://www.nourbese.com/). Audio recitation at: http://writing.upenn.edu/pennsound/x/ Philip.php

Rahim, Jennifer: "Haiti," which was previously published in *The Caribbean Writer* (Volume 25, 2011). Copyright © 2011 Jennifer Rahim. Reprinted with permission of the poet.

Robinson, Reihana: "On Our Knees or Homage to the Potato," previously published in *Ora Nui 2012: Māori Literary Journal* (Anton Blank Ltd, 2012). Copyright © 2012 Reihana Robinson. Reprinted with permission of the poet (reihanarobinson.co.nz).

Ross, W. W. E.: "The Diver," from *Shapes and Sounds: Poems of W. W. E. Ross* (Longman Canada Limited, 1968). Copyright © 1968 Mary Lowrey Ross. Reprinted with permission of the poet's family.

Scott, Dennis: "Epitaph," previously published in *The Penguin Book of Caribbean Verse in English* (Penguin, 1986). Permission granted by Joy R. Scott, Executor, Estate of Dennis C. Scott.

Senior, Olive: "Peppercorn," from *Shell* (Insomniac Press, 2007). Copyright © 2007 Olive Senior. Reprinted with permission of the poet (www.olivesenior.com).

Seth, Vikram: "For Philippe Honoré" and "Sampati," previously published in *The HarperCollins Book of English Poetry*, edited by Sudeep Sen (HarperCollins Publishers India, 2011). Reprinted with permission of the poet.

Shirley, Tanya: "A West Indian Poem," from *She Who Sleeps With Bones* (Peepal Tree Press, 2009). Reprinted with permission of the publisher.

Slessor, Kenneth: "Five Bells," from *One Hundred Poems, 1919–1939* (Angus & Robertson, 1944), more recently in Collected Poems, edited by Dennis Haskell and Geoffrey Dutton (Angus & Robertson / HarperCollins, 1994). Reprinted with permission of HarperCollins Australia.

Smith, Marty: "The Stolen," previously published in *Kaupapa: New Zealand Poets, World Issues*, edited by Hinemoana Baker and Maria McMillan (The Development Resource Centre, 2007). Copyright © 2007 Marty Smith. Reprinted with permission of the poet.

Sole, Kelwyn: "Conjunction," from *The Blood of Our Silence* (Ravan Press, 1988); "Blessing," from Projections in the Past Tense (Ravan Press, 1992); and "Housing Targets," from *Love That Is Night* (Gecko, 1998). All copyright © 2014 Kelwyn Sole. Reprinted with permission of the poet.

Stoneking, Billy Marshall: "The Seasons of Fire," from *Singing the Snake* (Angus & Robertson, 1990). Copyright © 1990 Billy Marshall Stoneking. Reprinted with permission of the poet (http://stonekingpages.webs.com/singingthesnake.htm).

Subramaniam, Arundhathi: "Epigrams for Life After Forty," from *Where I Live: New and Selected Poems* (Bloodaxe Books, 2009), reprinted with permission of the poet and the publisher; and "How Some Hindus Find Their Personal Gods," previously published in *The HarperCollins Book of English Poetry*, edited by Sudeep Sen (HarperCollins Publishers India, 2011), reprinted with permission of the poet (http://arundhathisubramaniam.webs.com/).

Sullivan, Robert: "Waka 99," from *Star Waka* (Auckland University Press, 1999. Reprinted with permission of the poet and the publisher. (Audio recitation at: http://www.poetryarchive.org/poetryarchive/singlePoem.do?poemId=16256)

Tiwoni, Habib: "'Pon Top Bluebeard Castle Hill," previously published in *Yellow Cedars Blooming: An Anthology of Virgin Islands Poetry* (Virgin Island Humanities Council, 1998). Reprinted with permission of the poet.

Tuwhare, Hone: "No Ordinary Sun," from *No Ordinary Sun* (Blackwood and Longman Paul, 1964). Reprinted with permission of the Hone Tuwhare Trust and the poet's family (http://honetuwhare.org.nz/).

Uppal, Priscila: "Books Do Hold Me at Night" and "Identity Crisis," previously published in *The HarperCollins Book of English Poetry*, edited by Sudeep Sen (HarperCollins Publishers India, 2011). Reprinted with permission of the poet (http://prisciLauppal.ca/).

van Wyk, Chris: "In Detention," from *It Is Time To Go Home* (Ad Donker, 1972). Reprinted with permission of the poet.

Walcott, Derek: "Adios, Carenage," from "The Schooner *Flight*," from *The Poetry of Derek Walcott 1948–2013*, edited by Glyn Maxwell (Farrar, Straus and Giroux, 2014). Copyright © 2014 Derek Walcott. Reprinted with permission of the publisher.

Wevill, David: "Diamonds," from *To Build My Shadow a Fire: The Poetry and Translations of David Wevill*, edited by Michael McGriff (Truman State University Press, 2010). Copyright © 2010 David Wevill. Reprinted with permission of the poet.

Wilkinson, Anne: "Lens," from *Heresies: The Complete Poems of Anne Wilkinson, 1924–1961*, edited by Dean Irvine (Signal Editions Poetry Series, Véhicule Press, 2004). Reprinted with permission of the publisher.

Williams, Marvin E.: "Noontide, Fort Christian," previously published in *Yellow Cedars Blooming: An Anthology of Virgin Islands Poetry* (Virgin Island Humanities Council, 1998). Copyright © 1998 Marvin E. Williams and the Virgin Island Humanities Council. Reprinted with permission of the poet's literary executor.

Wright, Judith: "Legend," from *A Human Pattern: Selected Poems* (Angus & Robertson Publishers, 1990; ETT Imprint / Imprint Classics, 2009; Fyfield Books / Carcanet, 2010). Copyright © 1990 Judith Wright. Used with permission of ETT Imprint and the poet's family.

P O E T R Y

F O U N D A T I O N

HARRIET MONROE POETRY INSTITUTE
Poets in the World series

Publications

· · · · ·

ILYA KAMINSKY, 2011–2013, HMPI DIRECTOR
Poets in the World series editor

Another English: Anglophone Poems from Around the World
edited by Catherine Barnett and Tiphanie Yanique
(Tupelo Press)

Elsewhere
edited by Eliot Weinberger
(Open Letter Books)

Fifteen Iraqi Poets
edited by Dunya Mikhail
(New Directions Publishing)

"Landays: Poetry of Afghan Women"
edited by Eliza Griswold
(*Poetry* magazine, June 2013)

New Cathay: Contemporary Chinese Poetry
edited by Ming Di
(Tupelo Press)

Open the Door: How to Excite Young People about Poetry
edited by Dorothea Lasky, Dominic Luxford, and Jesse Nathan
(McSweeney's)

Pinholes in the Night: Essential Poems from Latin America
edited by Raúl Zurita and Forrest Gander
(Copper Canyon Press)

Seven New Generation African Poets
edited by Kwame Dawes and Chris Abani
(Slapering Hol Press)

Something Indecent: Poems Recommended by Eastern European Poets
edited by Valzhyna Mort
(Red Hen Press)

The Star by My Head: Poets from Sweden
coedited and translated by Malena Mörling and Jonas Ellerström
(Milkweed Editions)

The Strangest of Theatres: Poets Writing Across Borders
edited by Jared Hawkley, Susan Rich, and Brian Turner
(McSweeney's)

KATHARINE COLES, HMPI INAUGURAL DIRECTOR

Blueprints: Bringing Poetry into Communities,
edited by Katharine Coles
(University of Utah Press)

Code of Best Practices in Fair Use for Poetry
created with American University's Center for Social Media
and Washington College of Law

Poetry and New Media: A Users' Guide
report of the Poetry and New Media Working Group
(Harriet Monroe Poetry Institute)

Other Books from Tupelo Press

See our complete backlist at www.tupelopress.org

CPSIA information can be obtained
at www.ICGtesting.com
Printed in the USA
FSOW01n0943200617
35404FS